FRED ROGERS

FRED ROGERS

THE LAST INTERVIEW

and OTHER CONVERSATIONS

with an introduction by DAVID BIANCULLI

MELVILLE HOUSE
BROOKLYN • LONDON

CONTENTS

INTRODUCTION

DAVID BIANCULLI

Fred Rogers.

Is there another name you could mention, especially in the field of popular entertainment in general and television in particular, so guaranteed to generate a wistful smile and a fond memory? Fred Rogers, the man who created and starred in the classic public television children's series *Mister Rogers' Neighborhood*, was a soft-spoken and caring person on TV—and was precisely the same when not on camera. Since his death in 2003, Rogers has been saluted, remembered, and even lionized by a series of movies, documentaries, and biographies. All of them attest to his powerful impact not only on the history of television but also on virtually every individual, from the youngest child to the most jaded adult, Rogers met in person.

Actor Tom Hanks, arguably the most warmly regarded actor of his generation, played Rogers in the 2019 movie *A Beautiful Day in the Neighborhood*. Director Morgan Neville celebrated him in his 2018 documentary, *Won't You Be My Neighbor?*, and Maxwell King researched, and wrote about, him at great length in his 2018 biography, *The Good Neighbor: The Life and Work of Fred Rogers*. All of those works are exemplary, and each reached the same conclusion: Rogers was "a man who seemed too good to be true—but was," in the words of Barbara Vancheri's *Pittsburgh Post-Gazette* review of King's book. Generous quotes from Rogers informed that book, just as footage of him on TV and elsewhere informed Neville's documentary, and Rogers's essence informed Hanks's portrayal. But one of the best ways to get to know Fred Rogers the person—what he thought, what he felt, why he made the TV programs he did—is to hear him at length, discussing his life and career in intimate, extended conversations with interviewers who have done their homework, and are equally adept at asking questions and listening and reacting to the answers.

This collection has several of the very best, ranging from Fred Rogers's 1985 interview with *Fresh Air* host Terry Gross (conducted when that show was a local public radio program in Philadelphia, two years before *Fresh Air* went national on NPR) to another revealing radio conversation, Rogers's 2002 interview with the host of *The Diane Rehm* show, originating from NPR's Washington, DC station, WAMU. That would be his last interview. But this collection also includes a 1995 phone interview conducted by songwriter and National Book Award–winner Phil Hoose, a 1999 interview with Karen

Herman for the Television Academy Foundation's Oral History collection, and a 2000 interview profile by *The Pittsburgh Post-Gazette* TV critic Rob Owen, catching Rogers as he was about to shoot the final installments of his long-running children's series. And all of these are preceded by a transcript of what may be the most important television appearance Fred Rogers ever made—in 1969, as the final witness called to testify before the US Senate Commerce Committee's Subcommittee on Communications.

Fred Rogers sat at the witness table in front of Subcommittee Chair John Pastore, a Democratic senator from Rhode Island who already had held TV to task by instigating an inquiry into the frequency of televised violence and its possible effects on children. In this case, Pastore was conducting a subcommittee hearing to determine whether the $20 million funding for public television, approved by President Lyndon Johnson before the 1968 election, should be maintained now that Richard Nixon, less persuaded of the potential and benefits of public TV, had been elected president. Fred Rogers was the last witness, and came with a written statement to read to the gruff chairman—but decided, instead, to speak to Pastore directly and quietly, man to man, and explain, simply and by quoting some of his own song lyrics, his vision of how television could positively affect young viewers. About six minutes later, after Rogers was through talking, Pastore said Rogers's testimony gave him "goosebumps." Reading the transcript, you may feel a similar reaction.

* * *

As for the interviews selected by the editor for this collection, each of them brings something special to this Fred Rogers party. The Terry Gross conversation took place when he had three decades of children's TV behind him, and a couple more to go. I started working for and with Terry on *Fresh Air* the very year this interview was conducted, in 1985, and am proud to still be part of the program. Terry is renowned as one of the finest interviewers in all of broadcasting, and you can see how easily she elicits memories and feelings from Rogers. Their conversation goes into depth about his early days in television, which were television's early days as well, and Terry unearths some fascinating details. Instead of joining the ministry as planned after graduating from college, Rogers started working for NBC's New York TV station, rising from lowly network page to a slightly less low production assistant on such network shows as *The Hit Parade*. But then, answering his own calling about how to serve children through this new medium, he moved to Pittsburgh in 1953 and got a job working at the city's brand-new public television station, WQED. How new was it? He tells Terry that he was one of only a handful of employees when he arrived there—and the station didn't even begin broadcasting for another five months. Amazing. And Rogers also recalls the spontaneous, "inspired" accident that led to him becoming a puppeteer, and introducing the still-beloved (and now animated, in a TV show of his own) character named Daniel Striped Tiger.

Phil Hoose comes at Fred Rogers from a different perspective. Hoose establishes Rogers's basic biography and early achievements—working on the local Pittsburgh series *The Children's Corner* with host Josie Carey (as described in detail

to Terry Gross), being ordained as a Presbyterian minister in
1962, starting his own children's TV show, *Mister Rogers,* for
Canadian television in 1963, and starting his own US public
TV series in 1968. But Hoose, among his many other achievements, is a musician, and he prods Fred Rogers to explain
where his love of music came from—eliciting wonderful stories about his family. Hoose, when talking to Rogers about
his early NBC days, gets Rogers to reveal some little-known
but fascinating tidbits. Rogers, it turns out, not only was a
floor manager on the musical variety series *The Hit Parade,*
but served as an assistant on NBC's famous 1951 live telecast
of the first opera commissioned and written specifically for
television, Gian Carlo Menotti's *Amahl and the Night Visitors.* More than forty years later, Rogers remembers a warm
exchange at the dress rehearsal between composer Menotti
and NBC Symphony Orchestra conductor Arturo Toscanini.
Before the live debut of Menotti's opera, according to Rogers,
Toscanini gave the composer a big hug—and, in Italian, an
equally big compliment. Amazing.

Karen Herman, as part of her oral history interview with
Fred Rogers for the Television Academy Foundation, catches
him near the end of his career, where he's reflective not only
about his show and career, but larger issues, including how
television can be of true service to young viewers. Those with
even a cursory understanding of Rogers and his approach to
TV and to children will not be surprised by the maxim he
was given at the start of his career by a trusted adviser, Margaret McFarland: "Whatever is mentionable is manageable."
But readers of this collection may be unexpectedly delighted
by his admission, to Herman, that he sees episodes of his old

series, after all these years, "like an old, classic book"—something that parents who got enjoyment from it when they were young end up sharing it with their own children. Fred Rogers is delighted by his own analogy, and a bit touched by it as well. Oh, and another surprise from the same conversation: Rogers reveals that one of his New Year's Day traditions was to phone Bob Keeshan, the former host of the CBS children's series *Captain Kangaroo,* every year to start the New Year, and compare what they both thought of the previous one. Again: Amazing.

Rob Owen, like Terry Gross, is someone I've known for decades—and when he came onto the beat as one of the "new wave" of television critics, he established an immediate reputation as a talented young TV critic whose writing style, research, critical skills, and perspective were among the very best. The only part of that to have changed, in the intervening decades, is that, like the rest of us, he's no longer quite so young. But while covering and watching Rogers and his TV programs while writing for *The Pittsburgh Post-Gazette,* Owen had a hometown advantage and perspective, but he also knew television and its history enough to recognize what a treasure he had in Rogers, and what an honor to catch him as he was taping the final five installments of *Mister Rogers' Neighborhood,* completing a run spanning thirty-three seasons and nearly one thousand individual episodes. Owen revisits the inaugural installment of Rogers's landmark children's program, noting the elements that made it special from the start. Owen checks in with another TV expert and historian, Robert Thompson (director of the Center for the Study of Popular Television at Syracuse University), who says—quite rightly—that Fred Rogers is one of the few TV pioneers, along with the likes of Ernie Kovacs and Steve Allen, who understood intuitively the power and potential of the medium of television. Then Owen visits Rogers's office to have a cozy conversation with the man himself, one that looks ahead as well as back, and distills some of the life lessons he's acquired over his fifty-year television career. "One of the greatest gifts you can give anybody," he tells Owen, "is the gift of your honest self."

And to end this compilation, there's Diane Rehm's radio interview from *The Diane Rehm Show* in 2002—the "last interview" that gives this volume its title. Among the many touching moments in this most recent radio transcript is one exchange in which Rehm describes a conversation with her son about his memories of watching *Mister Rogers' Neighborhood* every night with her and his sister. It's exactly the sort of cross-generational sharing Rogers was describing to Herman in their interview—and sort of puts everything in a wider perspective. So does a shocker of sorts, when Rogers is discussing the model of caring and loving for others exemplified by his grandparents—who, he tells her, set up an auxiliary hospital in the armory of their small town in 1918, to help care for overflow patients from the local hospital's incoming masses of people stricken ill that year with the flu epidemic. When he told Rehm that in 2002, there was no modern parallel to either that dire situation or that generous an act of kindness. Now there is.

Kindness, as much as anything, is the common thread in all these interviews and transcripts—the river that runs through them all. It also runs though the more recent samples and examinations of the life and impact of Fred Rogers: King's biography, Neville's documentary, and the biopic starring Hanks.

And, I'm very happy to report, it also holds true, quite recently, with the person who knew Rogers best: Joanne Rogers, to whom Fred proposed when they were both twenty-four years old. They were married from 1952 until his death in 2003, and I got to know her a little since then—well enough to ask her, during a 2018 interview about all the then-upcoming Fred Rogers tributes and movies, a potentially impertinent question. Our phone conversation took place a few months after the Harvey Weinstein allegations that brought the #MeToo movement into the mainstream conversation as one public media figure after another was accused of one serious indiscretion or another. Basically, I told her I'd be crushed if it ever came out that Fred had done something untoward or scandalous, and I needed her to tell me it was never going to happen.

Instead of resenting the question, Joanne just laughed—long and loudly. "Fred was love," she told me. "Fred was care. He loved women. He was truly a liberated man, and I used to tell him that. No, there won't be anything like that," she promised, laughing again at the very idea. "He really cares too much about people."

Everything you're about to read in this volume attests to that. Enjoy—and be inspired, all over again.

FRED ROGERS

TESTIMONY BEFORE THE U.S. SENATE COMMERCE COMMITTEE'S SUBCOMMITTEE ON COMMUNICATIONS

INTERVIEW BY SUBCOMMITTEE CHAIR
SENATOR JOHN PASTORE
UNITED STATES CONGRESS, SENATE
MAY 1, 1969

HARTFORD N. GUNN, JR: Now, Mr. Rogers is certainly one of the best things that's ever happened to public television, and his Peabody Award is testimony to that fact. We in public television are proud of Fred Rogers, and I'm proud to present Mr. Rogers to you now.

SENATOR JOHN PASTORE: All right, Rogers, you've got the floor. [*laughter*]

FRED ROGERS: Senator Pastore, this [*indicating document*] is a philosophical statement and would take about ten minutes to read, so I'll not do that. One of the first things that a child learns in a healthy family is trust. And I trust what you have said, that you will read this. It's very important to me; I care deeply about children. My first children—

PASTORE: Would it make you happy if you read it?

ROGERS: I'd just like to talk about it, if it's all right. My first children's program was on WQED fifteen years ago, and its budget was thirty dollars. Now, with the help of the Sears-Roebuck Foundation and National Educational Television as well as all of the affiliated stations, each station pays to show our program. It's a unique kind of funding in educational television. With this help, now our program has a budget of $6,000. It may sound like quite a difference. But $6,000 pays for less than two minutes of cartoons. Two minutes of animated . . . what I sometimes say bombardment. I'm very much concerned, as I know you are, about what's being delivered to our children in this country. And I've worked in the field of child development for six years now, trying to understand the inner needs of children. We deal with such things as—as the inner drama of childhood. We don't have to bop somebody over the head to make him—to make drama on the screen. We deal with such things as getting a haircut, or the feelings about brother and sisters, and the kind of anger that arises in simple family situations. And we speak to it constructively.

PASTORE: How long a program is it?

ROGERS: It's a half hour every day. Most channels schedule it in the noontime as well as in the evening. WETA here has scheduled it in the late afternoon.

PASTORE: Could we get a copy of this, so that we can see it? Maybe not today, but I'd like to see the program.

ROGERS: I'd like very much for you to see it.

PASTORE: I'd like to see the program itself, or any one of them.

ROGERS: We made a hundred programs for EEN, the Eastern Educational Network, and then when the money ran out, people in Boston and Pittsburgh and Chicago all came to the floor and said, "We've got to have more of this neighborhood expression of care." And this is what . . . this is what I give. I give an expression of care, every day, to each child. To help him realize that he is unique. I end the program by saying, "You've made this day a special day, by just your being you. There's no person in the whole world like you. And I like you just the way you are." And I feel that if we in public television can only make it clear that *feelings* are mentionable and manageable, we will have done a great service for mental health. I think that it's much more dramatic that two men could be working out their feelings of anger, much more dramatic than showing something of gunfire. I'm constantly concerned about what our children are seeing. And for fifteen years I have tried in this country and Canada to present what I feel is a *meaningful* expression of care.

PASTORE: Do you narrate it?

ROGERS: I'm the host, yes. And I do all the puppets and I write all the music and I write all the scripts.

PASTORE: Well, I'm supposed to be a pretty tough guy, and this is the first time I've had goose bumps for the last two days.

ROGERS: Well I'm grateful, not only for your goose bumps, but for your interest in our kind of communication. Could I tell you the words of one of the songs, which I feel is very important?

PASTORE: Yes.

ROGERS: This has to do with that good feeling of control, which I feel that children need to know is there. And it starts out, "What do you do with the mad that you feel?" And that first line came straight from a child. I work with children, doing puppets in very personal communication with small groups. "What do you do with the mad that you feel, when you feel so mad you could bite? / When the whole wide world seems oh so wrong, and nothing you do seems very right? / What do you do? Do you punch a bag? / Do you pound some clay or some dough? / Do you round up friends for a game of tag or see how fast you go? / It's great to be able to stop when you planned a thing that's wrong. / And be able to do something else instead, and think this song: / I can stop when I want to. / Can stop when I wish. / Can stop, stop, stop anytime. / And what a good feeling to feel like this! / And know that the feeling is really mine. / Know that there's something deep inside that helps us become what we can. / For a girl can be someday a lady, and a boy can be someday a man."

PASTORE: I think it's wonderful. I think it's wonderful. [*sighs*] Looks like you just earned the twenty million dollars. [*laughter and applause*]

INTERVIEW WITH FRED ROGERS

INTERVIEW BY TERRY GROSS
FRESH AIR
APRIL 16, 1985

TERRY GROSS: Was there somebody in your life who was the kind of figure for you like you've become to so many children who would, you know, like, reassure you, and want to discuss things with you? Of course, you can't actually step out of the TV and discuss it with all the kids, but you offer that to them. Was there someone like that for you?

FRED ROGERS: I guess the closest person was my grandfather, Mr. McFeely. And, of course, we've named the Speedy Delivery man for him. We called him "Ding Dong" because he taught us that childhood rhyme, "Ding dong bell / pussy in the well." And everybody called him "Ding Dong." He was the kind of person who would really support your strivings for autonomy. And while my parents and my grandmother were naturally very concerned about my health and hazards around, he was the kind of person who, when I would walk on one of his stonewalls, for instance, and they would say, "Better get down," Ding Dong would say, "Oh, let the kid walk on the wall; he's got to learn to do things for himself."

GROSS: What were the things that really scared you when you were a child?

ROGERS: I think the most scary thing was, uh, was being alone and thinking that maybe nobody would come to get me. And I think that school, beginning school was tough for me; that's probably why I've done so much work for children in this area. I think, also, I was frightened of the doctor, and that's probably why I've made all those videotapes about helping children know what hospitalization is like before they go. Probably why I wrote that song, "I Like to Be Told," because I did. I liked to be told about things before I had to go do them.

GROSS: Did you like scary movies or books?

ROGERS: I can't remember.

GROSS: Did you go to the movies a lot?

ROGERS: I would go to the movies, uh, it's hard for me to remember. I remember a couple movies that . . . I liked Shirley Temple, and I liked those kinds of stories that, you know, she would always come out okay at the end. And I met Shirley Temple Black not too long ago, and I just sat beside her in awe. And I said, "You—" It was interesting because the first thing I said to her was, "You were one of my favorite people." She said, "Were?!" That was the first thing she said. And that really put me back. I expected her to say something about, you know, "I'm really glad I could have been part of your childhood." But all she said was, "*Were*? I *was* one of your favorite people?" Isn't that interesting?

GROSS: Yeah, it is. Did she diminish in your esteem after saying that?

ROGERS: Little bit. But I think that, so many people you put on pedestals when you see them from afar, and it's probably just not fair to expect them to be as wonderful as you thought they would be when you met them.

GROSS: What about when you were a teenager? Was that an uncomfortable experience, or were you . . . Did you feel like you fit in with everybody in high school, which is, I think, a pretty traumatic time for a lot of people when they're growing up.

ROGERS: It sure is. I think the teenage years are probably uncomfortable for everybody; it's just that some seem to be able to carry it off with more élan than others. But, uh, it was tough for me at the beginning. And then, I made a couple friends who found out that the core of me was okay. And one of them was the president, or the head of the football team. He later became my best friend in high school. But it was after the beginning of that friendship that I was more accepted in school. Then I became the editor of the yearbook and, finally, the president of the student council by the end of high school. But I was a . . . I was a very shy person going into high school.

GROSS: What did you think you were gonna be when you got out of school and started a professional career?

ROGERS: I thought I was going to be a diplomat and was thinking about going to a school for diplomacy. And then I changed my mind—and this was during college—I wanted to be a minister and was all set to go to seminary after college. But I saw this thing called television, and I saw people throwing pies in each other's faces and all kinds of demeaning behavior, and I thought, "I would really like to try my hand at that and see what I could do." And so, instead of going to the seminary, after graduation I got a job at NBC in New York and went there for two years before joining educational television.

GROSS: You worked on *The Hit Parade* and *The Kate Smith Hour*, I think . . .

ROGERS: Mm-hmm, *The Voice of Firestone* and all of those programs.

GROSS: It surprises me, I think, that you left for a fledgling station—a brand new station—in educational television, which was also new. It sounds like it was very risky to do that. Why did you make that switch?

ROGERS: I don't know. It was . . . Pittsburgh was closer to where I grew up. Maybe I wanted to, um, I had just gotten married in New York, and maybe I had wanted to go back; I'm not sure that's so. I think that it had to do with wanting to work with children. Because every day that I had off at NBC, I would go and visit a day care center or an orphanage or a hospital that cared for children. And I cannot tell you why. I'm sure it had very deep roots. But when I got to Pittsburgh, and there were only three or four of us working at QED then. We weren't even on the air. This was in November of '53, and we didn't go on the air until April of '54, [*pauses*] thirty years ago. One of the secretaries and I did a children's program together because nobody else wanted to do a children's program . . . but we were doing all of these other things as well. Each of us had a salary of seventy-five dollars a week. And out of our own pockets we bought all of the props for the program. And we called the program *The Children's Corner*. And it was on an hour every day. And I expected that I would play the organ for the hostess to sing, she would introduce all of the films, which I, as the producer, would get from all over the country. They had to be free because we didn't have any budget. Well, I didn't realize it, but those films were very brittle at times. And, of course, everything was live, and we'd be on the air and here would be a film showing, and it would break. We'd have to fill with something. And so, the night before we went on the air, Mrs. Dorothy Daniel, who was the general manager of the station, gave me a little tiger puppet. So I called him Daniel, for her. And when the first film broke, I just poked the puppet through—and this was just a very fanciful set, with drawings on it—and I just poked him through, and it happened to be a clock where I poked him through, and he just said, [*as Daniel Striped Tiger*] "Uh, it's 5:02, and Columbus discovered America in 1492." And that was the first thing that I ever said through puppetry on the air.

GROSS: Wow. [*laughs*]

ROGERS: But I just wanted you to know that necessity, there, was the mother of that invention. Because it hadn't been planned. And so much that is spontaneous is what can be truly inspired. And I feel that all that I've done, that's been really helpful and good, has been inspired.

GROSS: You went back to the seminary after doing children's programming for a while, right?

ROGERS: Well, I started with the station, and after we got that children's program going, it got to be so busy for us that the secretary and I both gave up all of our other duties to do *The Children's Corner.* As it got moving, the second year, I decided I would go to the seminary, so I went on my lunch hour and took courses, just one at a time, never expecting that I would graduate. Took me eight years, and I finally graduated and was ordained a minister in the Presbyterian Church.

GROSS: Obviously, you're very religious, but I don't think you . . . it's not a denominational program, and I'm sure that's intentional on your part.

ROGERS: It's far from denominational and far from overtly religious. The last thing in the world that I would want to do would be something that's exclusive. I would hate to think that a child would feel excluded from *The Neighborhood* by something that I said and did.

GROSS: Can I just ask you one more thing before we go? You know how a lot of adults always say, "God, I wish I was a child again." Do you ever wish you were five or ten or twelve?

ROGERS: Yes. But I'd like to be that with what I know now. And I think that I'd like that because there are a good many significant people in my life that I have lost through death, and I'd like to be able to talk with them again. And tell them some things that I wasn't able to tell them then. In fact, I'd like to be able to tell them, "You are special."

THE GIFT OF YOUR HONEST SELF: AN INTERVIEW WITH FRED ROGERS

INTERVIEW BY PHIL HOOSE

PASS IT ON!

SUMMER 1995

During the minute or so that I am on hold, waiting for Fred Rogers to pick up the phone, I grow increasingly tense. The next voice I hear will belong to a man whose sweater is in the Smithsonian, along with the Spirit of St. Louis and pterodactyl skeletons and Archie Bunker's chair. He is one of the most identifiable figures in American life. When he finally does answer, how many other callers will be on hold as I scramble for whatever I can get of his time?

And then the voice arrives and instantly everything is all right. It is a slow voice, offered with modulation and care. There are spaces between words and bigger spaces between sentences. The words themselves are simple. Time slows by the syllable. Fred Rogers speaks to me as he has spoken to my daughters and as he speaks to millions of children in homes and day care centers each morning, and with the same effect. I am certain that there is no one on earth with whom he would rather be talking. I am special. I am good. I am a Neighbor.

The interview becomes a conversation. I ask him a question and sometimes there is no answer at all for a while.

After it comes, often he wants to know what I think. "Is that the way it is for you?" he asks. "Do you agree?" he wonders. Assistants may be slipping him notes from all directions, but I sense that he really wants to know. If I offer a thought or an insight, he takes time to consider what I've said and finds ways to affirm something about it. The same care and humanity, the same basic regard for a person's worth, comes through the phone as comes through the screen. He is what he is. When one is with Fred Rogers in any medium, the message is clear: Together, as safely and calmly as possible, we're all in the Neighborhood.

Fred McFeely Rogers was born in 1928 in Latrobe, Pennsylvania. His family was involved in banking and manufacturing. He has one adopted sister, eleven years younger than he. Fred went to high school in Latrobe, then majored in music composition at Rollins College in Florida. After graduation in 1951, he was hired by NBC in New York and became a part of some of the most important and exciting programs in the early history of television, including *The Voice of Firestone*, *The Lucky Strike Hit Parade*, *The Kate Smith Hour*, and *The NBC Opera Theatre*.

In November of 1953 Fred moved to Pittsburgh to develop program schedules for WQED, the nation's first community-supported public television station. One of the programs he developed and produced was called *The Children's Corner*. It was a live, hour-long visit with Fred's puppets and host Josie Carey. Several later-to-be *Neighborhood* regulars were born on that show, including puppets Daniel Striped Tiger and King Friday XIII. During the seven years of *The Children's Corner* Fred began to study childhood development and also to attend the Pittsburgh Theological Seminary. He was ordained as a Presbyterian minister in 1962.

In 1963 Fred created a series called *Mister Rogers* for the Canadian Broadcasting Corporation. For the first time, he appeared on camera as the series host, and it was the precursor to the format he developed for *Mister Rogers' Neighborhood*, first distributed through PBS in 1968. Today, the program reaches more than seven million families each week and there are more than six hundred episodes in the series. *Mister Rogers' Neighborhood* is the longest-running children's program on public television. Fred Rogers has won nearly every children's television programming award available, including Emmys as a performer and as a writer.

According to *Neighborhood*'s press kit, the most important goal of the series is to "Encourage children to feel good about themselves." Often, he tells his young viewers that "You are the only person like you in the whole world," and "People can like you just because you're you." During an episode viewers visit both the "television house," in which Mr. Rogers talks with young viewers, shows them things of interest, and escorts them to places where everyday things are made or done; and the Neighborhood of Make-Believe, a mostly puppet kingdom in which Mr. Rogers never appears. It is a deliberate separation, intended to help children realize the difference between reality and fantasy.

It has always been a musical neighborhood. Fred Rogers has written over two hundred songs for children as well as thirteen musical stories. Often, segments are accompanied by the elegant piano of Johnny Costa, a nationally known jazz pianist.

This interview took place by phone from Fred Rogers's office in Pittsburgh. Fred discusses the challenge of maintaining an island of calm in a rapidly accelerating and often violent television environment. He talks about the role of music in his work and about his early life with music.

Fred lives with his wife in the Pittsburgh area. They are the parents of two married sons and are the grandparents of boys who were born in 1988 and 1993.

PHIL HOOSE: What are your early memories of music?

FRED ROGERS: One of the first is of my grandfather McFeely. We named Mr. McFeely, the Speedy Delivery person, after him. He loved to play the fiddle. I'll never forget the time I was able to accompany him on piano. His favorite song was "Play, Gypsy, Dance Gypsy, Play While You May." [*sings it*] I played the piano at his house and he played the fiddle. And to think that I am a grandfather now, and I have two grandchildren, six years old and two years old. The other night the two-year-old patted the piano bench, which meant that he wanted me to sit there and play. And when I play, I wish you could see him dance! He takes one foot and puts it down and sways and puts the other one down and sways back and forth. He's very musical, I think.

HOOSE: Did your parents sing to you when you were little?

ROGERS: I have a feeling that they did. They always told me stories about my listening to the radio and then I would either hum what I heard, or, after my grandmother McFeely bought me a piano, I would go to the piano and pick out the tunes that I had heard. So radio and books meant a lot to me too. There wasn't such a thing as television then. They remember taking me to movies when I was five or six. Then I would come home and play the songs from the movie. I always played by ear. I wanted to learn to play the organ, so my grandmother got me a Hammond organ. Evidently, when I was about ten, they put the speaker out on the porch on Christmas Eve, and I would play Christmas carols, and people would drive up and down the street and listen to the music.

HOOSE: By then you could harmonize your notes into chords?

ROGERS: Oh, sure. It took me a long time before I really learned to read notes well because it came so easily by ear. Do you play by ear?

HOOSE: Yes, I haven't learned to read [notes] yet. It seems hard. I've taken some swings at it but I haven't really learned. What gave you the sensitivity, the empathy that you have with children? What gave you the desire to help them feel strong and powerful?

ROGERS: Maybe being an only child for eleven years. Your antennae go out pretty far in trying to sense how other people are feeling. My sister didn't come along until I was eleven. I don't know; I'm sure some of it is biological. My parents were very much concerned about others. They were very active in their church. Both Mother and Dad were elders in the First Presbyterian Church of Latrobe for many years. I remember during the Second World War, my mother was in charge of the whole area's volunteer surgical dressing department. I understand that in World War I she helped make sweaters for soldiers. She was a great sweater maker. She made all my sweaters.

HOOSE: Including the famous one?

ROGERS: Yeah. Every month she would make a sweater. So at Christmas time, twelve of us in our extended family got a sweater each year that was made by Nancy Rogers. Every year we would open these boxes and here would be this wonderful sweater, and Mother would say, "Now what kind does everybody want next year?" She had all these patterns, you know. She'd say, "I know what kind you want, Freddy. You want the one with the zipper up the front." And that's what she made. The one that's in the Smithsonian is one that she had made.

HOOSE: How did you land in the fast lane in New York in the early days of television?

ROGERS: Well, I had just gotten a music degree from Rollins College. I was a composition major. When I decided I wanted to do television and got a job at NBC in New York, they noticed I had a degree in music so they assigned me to various music programs. What a wonderful experience that was! *The Hit Parade, The Kate Smith Hour, The Voice of Firestone, The NBC Opera Theater* . . . those were all programs that I was intimately associated with.

HOOSE: What did you do on a show like *The Lucky Strike Hit Parade?*

ROGERS: I was a floor manager. Now, that was a huge program. We had five floor managers. I had earphones on, and I was connected to the television director who was in a booth. And the director was telling me what is coming up next and to get it ready. Then you ask the stagehands to move things and get them prepared for the next scene. And you also ask the talent to get into place and you tell them how long they have until the next scene is about to start. I remember Snooky Lanson, one of the stars, so well. Do you know who I mean?

HOOSE: No.

ROGERS: He was one of the stars. There was Dorothy Collins, and June Valley, and Russell Arms, and Snooky Lanson. They were the stars during my two years. Anyway, Mr. Lanson loved to play craps backstage with the stagehands. I'd go back there and say, [*whispers*] "Mr. Lanson, you're ON in two minutes." He'd say, "Be right there, Freddy." And so he'd come out and get in place and it was as if he'd been right there all evening. It was just amazing what could be done in the days of live television. We started rehearsing early in the morning and by nine o'clock at night it was ready to go on the air. *The NBC Opera Theater* was what I really loved. We did the first *Amahl and the Night Visitors.* It was commissioned for that program. I remember Toscanini coming to the dress rehearsal, and after he just hugged Gian Carlo Menotti [the composer] and said in Italian, "It's the best you've ever done!"

Here I was. How did I know I was right in the middle of history being made?

HOOSE: Did you have any sense of that?

ROGERS: No. In fact, I would go home and tell JoAnne—we were married when I was in New York, in the second of those two years—I didn't know anything about famous people, except Menotti. I remember one day saying, "Oh, Sarah"—I usually call her Sarah—"there was this *wonderful* singer. She really is going to go far. Her name is Peggy Lee." Sarah said, "Fred, she already has gone far." But these were people I was floor managing. I was hearing wonderful music.

HOOSE: Did you, as a musician yourself, want to write pop songs in those days?

ROGERS: Oh, yes. In fact, I'd think, "Here you are, right in Tin Pan Alley, and you're managing other people's music." Once when I was in college some people I knew got me introduced to Jack Lawrence. He was one of the biggest songwriters in New York. He wrote "If I Didn't Care" and a lot of other songs. He was like Irving Berlin, that big. I went to visit him when I was a freshman. And I had five songs. I went to his brownstone. He was very welcoming. He asked me to play my songs, and I did. He listened, and he said, "Those songs have a lot of promise, Fred. How many more do you have?" I said, "A few." He said, "Well, to me a few means three, so that makes eight. I'd like you to come back when you have a barrel full." I was crestfallen. I was sure my five songs would end up on Broadway. But that was some of the best advice I ever got.

HOOSE: It seems contrary to what you hear now. Everyone says, "Only bring a publisher or an agent your best song" or "Only bring a few."

ROGERS: I can understand that if you have already written your barrel full. He was telling me to write, write, write. It was excellent advice. The more I wrote the more I saw the possibility of writing. I don't know that I would ever have written these little operas for the *Neighborhood* if I hadn't gotten that advice then. In other words, "Don't ever think of any one composition as so precious that it has to define you."

HOOSE: So did you ever go back with your barrel full?

ROGERS: I did, when I was already doing my *Neighborhood* programs. He had heard them on television.

HOOSE: Have you ever formally studied the role of music in child development, or what characteristics of songs seem to appeal to children?

ROGERS: I used to take my puppets to the center where I did my practicum work in child development. I would show the children the puppets and talk for them and play music for them to dance or move to, or to make up words to. I rarely played ordinary nursery rhyme songs. I loved in front of them what I loved to do; that is, to make the puppets talk and play the piano. I think one of the greatest gifts you can give anybody is the gift of your honest self. The woman who was the director of that nursery school told me that she had never seen the children use puppets, and there were puppets all around. She said they used them imaginatively when I would come with my puppets. She made an analogy to a father of one of the children several years before. He was a sculptor. He would come to the school once a week just to fashion clay in the midst of the children, not to teach sculpting, but to show how you enjoy it in front of the children. He would come and love that clay in front of the children one day a week. She said that never before or since had the children used clay so imaginatively as when that man used to come and love it in front of them. Nothing didactic about it.

HOOSE: Just loving what you love in front of them . . .

ROGERS: Yes. They will catch your enthusiasm. Attitudes are caught, they're not taught.

HOOSE: As you say that, I think about what I love to do, and whether that's my experience. It's almost Zen-like. With music, if I'm singing a song or making one up with children, if I become too conscious of the process or the time, it's distracting and we lose each other. I think tension is caught as well. But I think when I'm having fun, they're having fun. We're all having fun.

ROGERS: So you caught my notion . . .

HOOSE: Why is music so important to your neighborhood?

ROGERS: Because it's essential to me. Doing puppets or playing the piano or making up songs isn't for everybody, but it's like drinking water or breathing fresh air for me. And *Neighborhood* would certainly be different if I weren't in it. And it would be fake if it didn't have a large musical component.

HOOSE: One of the things I love about your music is the jazz piano. Is it improvised?

ROGERS: I write the songs, and then Johnny Costa, a magnificent jazz pianist, improvises much of the music around them.

HOOSE: You use opera in your neighborhood. I've never heard that in children's entertainment except maybe with *Mighty Mouse*.

ROGERS: I've written about thirteen operas of about twenty minutes each. *The Grandparent's Opera* was one of them.

HOOSE: Do you keep up with children's music? Are you aware of the artists that are out there now?

ROGERS: I do not. I just give to children what I find within me. I don't watch much television at all, either. I'm a reader. We haven't used television well at all in this world. It's a perfectly wonderful medium. There have been times when it's been used beautifully. But it's been so misused that it bothers me.

HOOSE: Life and TV are noisier and more action oriented now than when you started working. Has this affected your show?

ROGERS: We're still one of the islands that encourage quiet and some space to think. We hear every day from people saying how grateful they are for some time of calm. Now, I think people should have complete silence every day.

    I just get so annoyed when I'm out somewhere and I can't close my ears the way I can close my eyes. We're bombarded from every direction. Who says that people want to hear what's broadcast in public?

HOOSE: I know what you mean. Our children do watch TV. We regulate how much and what they can see, but we let them watch. Our younger daughter, who is almost five, feels a lot of pressure at school to react to the *Power Rangers* and other faster, noisier shows.

ROGERS: I agree. My grandson has been sucked into that too. He watches the *Power Rangers*. But he still watches the *Neighborhood*. I just lament the fact that children watch so much. Too much. They need time to play.

HOOSE: Has all of this affected either how many children watch the *Neighborhood* or the age at which they leave you?

ROGERS: We used to think that the target age was five or six, and that we might have some four-year-olds and seven-year-olds. Now we're hearing that the children are starting to watch at eighteen months. The high point is about three. It's ridiculous. What's that doing to their psyche? I'm not concerned about what they might see on the *Neighborhood*, but I am concerned about what they might see all around it. Some children watch unmonitored and see shows meant for adults.

HOOSE: What is it like to be the remaining island of calm in a rising sea? Do you ever stand up there in front of the camera and feel like you've got to be a lot for a lot of people?

ROGERS: All I can do is be myself. I've had the grace to be able to do that. I walk into the studio and I think, "Let some word that is heard be Thine." Whatever doesn't come from the eternal is just dross anyway. So I just pass on what's been given to me.

HOOSE: Do you ever have visions as you look at the camera of the horrible situations some children are in as they look back at you?

ROGERS: Oh yes. Not that I have any exact view of it, but I think about the children and some of the ones I've known in desperate straits. I've been to a lot of places, some of them very poor. I know I can't do everything, but I know I can give the kind of nourishment that comes from an understanding of the development of the human personality.

HOOSE: Do you have a sense of the importance of being one of the only widely visible males that works with and cares about young children? Do you see yourself as a role model for maleness?

ROGERS: I remember one time after the *Neighborhood* had been on quite a while, the people in New York asked me to come talk about doing some commercial television. One of the first questions they asked me was "What costume will you wear?" They said, "You've got to jazz up what you do." I said, "Well, it looks to me as if this meeting is over," because for all the time I've been on television all I've ever wanted to do was to give one more honest adult to the children who are watching. Covering me up with all kinds of jazzy stuff is not my idea of the expression of honesty. Does that answer your question?

HOOSE: Part of it. I still want to ask about maleness. One reason many people appreciate you is that you give a child a chance to see a man on television who is not loud, or fast in his movements, or always in an action mode. To what extent is that just you, and to what extent do you see yourself as a role model?

ROGERS: I think that if I were very aggressive in my movements and my speech that it would be a sham for me to try to act like Mr. Rogers. We got a letter yesterday in which someone said how grateful they were that a certain person was on television who was close to being "Mr. Rogers-esque." It seems to have become part of the culture: that a gentle, calm, quiet male can be considered "Mr. Rogers-esque." I just don't think you can fake that. I wouldn't want to advise someone who is just the opposite of me to do it just like me. It wouldn't be real. I think children and adults long to be in touch with what's real. Don't you?

HOOSE: I do, and I think people "catch" realness just as they catch the love one has for the things one does.

ROGERS: That's a beautiful analogy, picking up on what we talked about before.

HOOSE: Has your being a minister affected the *Neighborhood*, or your work with children?

ROGERS: It has helped me become who I am, and it's all a part of me. My relationship with my Creator is just part of who I am. I don't think you have to use labels to allow people to see what is your inspiration.

HOOSE: You've been working with children for four decades now. Would you have any advice for those of us who are just now choosing to spend a good bit of our time and our creative energy working with children?

ROGERS: [*long silence*] First of all, I would think that it would be important to understand the roots of your desire to do that. As you come to understand that, then you can understand what might be in the children with whom you're communicating. With parents, for example, as a child goes through certain stages of development, that reevokes those feelings in their parents that stem from those same stages that they went through. I think that way you get to be more gentle with yourself, and as you're able to do that, then the children that you're with sense that you're accepting of them, as you become more accepting of who you have been as a child, that child that you continue to carry along with you in life.

"I'VE GOT THE GREATEST JOB IN THE WORLD"

INTERVIEW BY KAREN HERMAN
THE INTERVIEWS: AN ORAL HISTORY OF TELEVISION
TELEVISION ACADEMY FOUNDATION
JULY 22, 1999

KAREN HERMAN: Before we go on to *Mister Rogers,* one last question about *The Children's Corner.* What is your favorite memory of the show? Of a particular scene, of something that you did that you're very proud of on that show?

ROGERS: It's so hard to think of isolated moments. I think of one day, when Josie came from KDKA and she was really upset. I don't know what had happened; you know, things can happen in commercial television that maybe they don't happen so much in public broadcasting. At any rate, she came in—Ernie Coombs had started the program—and she came in and she just said to Daniel, "I am so upset." And Daniel said, [*as Daniel Striped Tiger*] "Well, you just tell me about it." And she just bared her soul to him. And this was so real, I mean, I wonder if she even knew that we were on the air, and the camera was on—she probably did. But she trusted Daniel's ears so, and she trusted her audience so, that she could be her whole self. And again, I suppose I've said it many, too many times, but this is such a personal medium, that that's what matters. Television has the chance of building a real community out of an entire country. It has a wonderful opportunity of doing that. We see that in times of crisis; it can really bring people together.

And now, there're many common memories. That's one of the things—one of the dividends about being on so long— is that children who grew up with the *Neighborhood* can be having children, and also grandchildren. It's like an old book; it's like an old, classic book. If your parents read a certain book to you that their parents read to them, and they had that warm feeling about being read to, they pass that on to their children, there isn't anything like that, as far as comfortable roots are concerned.

It's fun to be part of that kind of tradition. I never in a million years would've expected that I'd be sitting here talking with you about, about this after, well, 1951, in 2001, it'll be fifty years as part of this industry. [*laughs*]

HERMAN: Do you think the advent of cable has diluted that, so there'll be less commonality?

ROGERS: I don't know. All I hope for is that people will stick with a program that's really good—that it'll be supported over a long period of time, so those traditions can last. I would love to be able to offer—let me put it a different way. The boys and Joanne and I used to watch *The Waltons* every week that it was on. I think it would be wonderful if our kids, then, show it to their children. Because they would have the feeling that we had—maybe they wouldn't want to—but at least it'd be available.

HERMAN: Talk about putting [*Mister Rogers' Neighborhood*] together. You write the scripts?

ROGERS: Mm-hmm.

HERMAN: Talk about that process, picking the topics, the actual writing, who you consulted with.

ROGERS: Yes. Well, as long as Margaret [McFarland] was alive, she and I would talk about possible themes, and uh, I would always . . . I remember even when I was in Nantucket, I would call her. One time, we decided that we should write a song about permissible regression. You know, regression in the service of the ego. And I thought long and hard: "How can I do that?" And, I remember [it] coming to me in Nantucket. I called her up, and I said, "What do you think of this?!"

Sometimes you feel like holding your pillow / All night long. / Sometimes you hold your teddy bear tightly. / He's old, but he's still strong. / Sometimes you want to snuggle up closely with your own mom and dad at night / You even need the light sometimes / But that's not bad / Please don't think it's funny / When you want an extra kiss. / There are lots and lots of people / Who sometimes feel like this. / Please don't think it's funny / When you want the ones you miss / There are lots and lots of people / Who sometimes feel like this.

Well, she was so pleased. And the last verse—I mean, there are several verses—but I remember the last verse saying—and I remember, you know, writing this out in the work house, right there, at the lip of the sea. Oh, there's nothing better for me than being right beside the sea.

In the long, long, trip of growing / There are stops along the way / For thoughts of all the soft things / And a look at yesterday / For a chance to fill our feelings / With comfort and with ease / And then tell the new tomorrow / You can come now when you please / So please don't think it's funny / When you want an extra kiss. / There are lots and lots of people / Who sometimes feel like this. / Please don't think it's funny / When you want the ones you miss / There are lots and lots of people / Who sometimes feel like this.

Now, that's our response to what the people in the field of child development would say, "permissible regression": regression in the service of the ego. In other words, stepping back, and feeling that it's all right to do younger things in order for you to then later go forward.

HERMAN: Can you give me an example of how you would segue to that song?

ROGERS: We might have a theme in which King Friday and Queen Sarah have to go off somewhere to work for a whole weekend. And Chuck Aber would be the babysitter for Prince Tuesday, and they would have fun together until it was time to go to bed. And the prince was starting to feel . . . "I can't stay brave for this whole evening." And Chuck Aber would say: "Please don't think it's funny / When you want an extra kiss / Or the ones you miss / There are lots and lots of people / Who feel like this." And then that helps the prince know he's not alone in those feelings; it also help the people who are listening to what the prince and Chuck are saying to know that they're not alone. And that it's okay. Many children will do what adults might consider inappropriate things for their age when they happen to be feeling stressful. Well, all they're doing is going back to an earlier time to help their feelings at the moment. It doesn't mean they're going to stay there all the time; it just means that they're regrouping so that they can take the next step.

HERMAN: About the transition to the Land of Make-Believe via the trolley. There was a point where the trolley was sort of on its own, and you installed a switch. Why was that?

ROGERS: Yes. I wanted to show the children . . . Oh, early-on, I forgot to mention. Early on, I used to use a telescope, and I'd go like this, [*makes and extends telescope with his hands*] and the telescope would then dissolve into Make-Believe. I just remembered that! That was a long time ago.

But I wanted the children to see that everything in reality was real. So I showed them underneath, the switch that made the trolley work. Of course, once it goes to Make-Believe, then anything can happen. I mean, King Friday can come down in a parachute, as he did last week. [*laughs*]

HERMAN: Okay, let's talk a little bit about the Land of Make-Believe within the show: how it works with what you've been talking about in the beginning of the show.

ROGERS: Yes, I really feel that, uh, the opening reality of the program, we deal with the stuff that dreams are made of. And then, in the Neighborhood of Make-Believe, we deal with it as if it were a dream. And then, when it comes back to me, we deal with a simple interpretation of the dream.

It sounds very analytical, and it probably doesn't show it all, and that's fine; I hope it doesn't. But that's at least, when I'm writing the script, that's what I think about. And that anything can happen in Make-Believe. And we can talk about anything in reality.

Margaret used to say, "Whatever is mentionable is manageable." And I hope that children can get that from our work.

HERMAN: Let's talk about some of those mentionable things that you wouldn't necessarily think of as mentionable. You did a special when Robert Kennedy was assassinated. How did that come about?

ROGERS: Well, we stayed up all night 'cause—that, again was, uh, I think we did that live. I'm not sure—I think we did that for the network, live. At any rate, there had been too many things; the country was in deep grief. I mean, President Kennedy had been killed, then Martin Luther King was killed, and then Robert Kennedy, and I said, "I've got to talk to the families."

And so, as I remember, the theme of that program was my saying to the parents, "The best thing you can do is to include your children in your own ways of dealing with grief. Because your children will know, anyway, without your saying anything, how you're feeling. So, please, if it's going to church, or synagogue, or if it's going for a walk along a stream, whatever your way of dealing with grief is, please include your children." That was the main plea. And a lot of people felt that that was helpful. You know, to actually say, "Here we are," you know. "We're a country in grief. Now, we can, as a community, work through it."

HERMAN: And you did something very similar in the eighties with Ronald Reagan, and the Pope, and John Lennon after they faced assassination attempts, and in Lennon's case, was killed. You went on and did a similar program.

ROGERS: I forgot that. [*laughs*] Yeah. I do remember making the public service announcement for, for the war.

HERMAN: The Gulf War?

ROGERS: The Gulf War, yeah. And it, again, I think it was a plea for parents to, uh, to allow their children to know that they would do everything they could to keep their children safe. Because that's what children would be concerned about. There was all of this stuff on television about people getting killed and, you know, people in the direst of straits with [*gestures to his face*] visages that were tortured. And I understand that, and I understand why that would need to be shown. But if children happened to see that, they could be frightened terribly. In fact, news programs are probably the most frightening programs for anybody.

But, what I wanted the parents to know was that

invariably, when children see something like that, their first thought will be "What will happen to me?" So, you know, whether we could be absolutely sure of this fact or not, we need to say it: "I will take care of you." We need to say it.

HERMAN: So, the same would be true [about] the shows you've done on divorce?

ROGERS: Oh, sure. You know, my mother used to say, a long time ago, whenever there would be any really—catastrophe that was in the movies or on the air, she would say, "Always look for the helpers. There will always be helpers, just on the sidelines." That's why I think that if news programs could make a conscious effort of showing rescue teams, of showing medical people, anybody who is coming in to a place where there is a tragedy, to be sure that they include that. Because if you look for the helpers, you'll know that there's hope.

HERMAN: You also did a show on death.

ROGERS: Mm-hmm. One of my goldfish died, and I wanted the children to know that I had feelings about that kind of separation. And while you can't get very close to a goldfish, it can remind you of something or someone that you were close to. And so that's why I talked about my dog, Mitzi, and when she died, and how I cried, and how my grandmother comforted me. You know, it's just a matter of being honest with the children, and whoever happens to be watching with the children.

But if you had told me, for instance, twenty-five years

ago, that I would have done a whole week on divorce, for instance, or on childcare, I would've thought, that's beyond my belief! That's beyond my ken. But, divorce is so prevalent, and if you're not affected directly, you're certainly affected indirectly in school, or on the playground, so we did do a whole week about divorce. And Prince Tuesday was very concerned, because his mother and dad were angry with each other, that they were gonna get a divorce. And that was how it was dealt with in Make-Believe, but then, we had some real instances in reality. And then, childcare, I mean, many children, nowadays, are participating in childcare, who weren't twenty-five years ago.

HERMAN: And what is the major concern of a child, about childcare?

ROGERS: Well, being taken, and will somebody come and get them. And what happens when their parents leave them, and do their parents think about them while they're gone? And is it all right to think about their parents themselves, when the parents are gone? That kind of thing.

HERMAN: Have you ever talked about television?

ROGERS: [*nods*] Just last week, we did a program in which I read a book, actually, that I had—I took the children to the library, and showed them how books are taken out of the library. Showed them some of the things that happen in a library, like a man teaching chess and another man helping children with crafts, and I love this library, it's the Homewood

Library in Pittsburgh; it's just wonderful. At any rate, they could see that I loved the library—but the book that was involved in that program was called *The Day the TV Broke*.

And it's this whole book, a picture book, about what happens when the TV breaks, and the little boy is very glum: nothing to do. Well, of course, what happens is that he finds all of these things to do. His father carts the TV set away, brings it back at the end of the week, and the kid is too busy with other things to even look at it right away. Wonderful theme, you know. In fact, our grandsons—we have two grandsons—and they're at the summer place, where there is no television. This is a house that we've had for forty years, and I said, "There's one thing we must never have in the house, and that's television."

And so, they're there, and ordinarily they watch a lot of television at home. I heard from their mother that they're not missing it at all. You know, they're doing lots of other things. And that's a great lesson for us. We don't have to have this sound and picture twenty-four hours a day. If I could just get people—you know—just turn off *The Neighborhood*, turn off whatever's there and play. You know, use this, [*points to his head*] the best of all.

HERMAN: You've done a number of shows demystifying television, even your show.

ROGERS: Sure, I've said to the cameras, "Please pull back and show that this is a set," and I walk right off the porch and off into the studio and show the little model. People like that—people like—somebody said to me, "Why do you suppose that people have watched *The Neighborhood* for so long?" I said, "People love honesty. They like to be in touch with those who are honest and real." Don't you? I mean, don't you like to be with real people? People who aren't afraid to make mistakes, people who just know that life is a gift, and relish in it? Yeah. [*laughs*]

HERMAN: Let's talk about mistakes for a moment. If you make a mistake while you're filming, do you sometimes leave them in?

ROGERS: Mm-hmm. You may have seen the program in which Sylvia Earle came and showed—we were going to demonstrate to the children this aqua sound thing. I wanted to show the children how fish actually make noise underwater, because, of course, it's not anything we hear. So Sylvia put—you know who Sylvia Earle is? She's the sort of, the present Jacques Cousteau—she's the last word when it comes to underwater stuff. In fact, we're gonna tape with her probably in either September or October in these submergibles. They're just individual submarines. So we'll have—she'll be in one, and I'll be in the next, and we'll be goin' along [*demonstrates with his hands*]—anyway. She came, and we put this thing into the tank, and you couldn't hear a thing. The fish weren't "speaking," I guess.

And so we went through it, and she said, "Well, that's that," and I knew that later in the program, I had a film about it anyway, so I just said, "Well sometimes, things just don't

work." And she said, "Yeah, that's right." And so we ended
the scene, and people said, "Well, I guess you wanna do that
again," and I said, "No, I don't. I want the children to see that
even with adults, sometimes it doesn't work out the way you
planned." So, that's in the program. [*laughs*] The fish don't
make any sounds.

HERMAN: You often, when you're speaking, you ask people
to take ten seconds and think about the people that helped
them along the way. What kind of reactions have you gotten
from that?

ROGERS: Just wonderful. I think silence is one of the greatest gifts that we have. You know, here, I've been talking with
you for hours. And I think that if I would just stop, there
would be a chance for people to think, "What's going on?"
and maybe go deeper within themselves.

I started this, this gift of silence, in a commencement
speech, I believe, quite a while ago. And one time, when I
was at the White House for the Conference on Children and
Television, they asked me to make a presentation, and I did.
And both the Clintons and both the Gores were there, and,
well, almost everybody in children's broadcasting. And I, at
that time, gave a whole minute of silence. And after that meeting was over, I was walking out, and one of the guards—you
know, the military guards at the White House [*sits up straight*]
all in white and gold—one of the guards came up to me and
said, "Thank you, Mr. Rogers." And I said, "For what?" and he
said, "For that silence." And I said, "Well, who did you think
about?" 'Cause I said, "Please take a minute to think about
those who have helped you become who you are." He said, "I

thought about my grandfather's brother, who, just before he died, took me to his basement and gave me his fishing pole." He said, "I hadn't thought about it in a long time. But I love fishing, and I know that must have come from him."

So maybe you'll have some nice, blank tape for whoever is doing research, to take some time to think about those who have cared so deeply for you that you're really nourished in this whole life because of knowing them. [*pauses and looks at Herman and the camera; silence*]

HERMAN: Who do you think about?

ROGERS: Well, it's not unlikely that I would think about my grandfather McFeely, and uh, and my grandmother, and my parents, and Jim Stumbaugh, and then, those who are still living—the people that I work with. You know, when I pray in the morning, there's such a long list of people, it would probably take three legal pads of paper, single-spaced, to tell you all the people who mean so much to me in this world and in the world beyond. I pray for their spirits—I've [been] thinking about Jack Heinz a lot since this Kennedy accident, because he was killed in an airplane accident, too. A bizarre accident in which a helicopter was trying to do something to the bottom of his plane, in flight, and his plane crashed. But, you ask about the beginnings of Family Communications, he was on our very first board and loved the work that we did. We have a wonderful board of directors now, and always have had, but, I don't know what it is about loss, and the memory of loss, that can help people go deeper and deeper within themselves. I guess, everybody—because everybody's—it's because nobody is immune to loss.

And, you know, I've had people walk up to me after we taped that segment in New York with Maya Lin; I was walking down the street in Manhattan, and people would walk up to me and without even stopping, would say such things as, "Thank you for my childhood." [*pause*] It's such a fabulous thing to walk through this life with this face. [*laughs*] The things that—people have such trust that I will respond in a caring way, that—well, how can I say how grateful I am for what I've been able to do and be. How can I ever express my gratitude enough?

HERMAN: Then again, people trust you because you come through, so—two-way street.

ROGERS: [*considers this*] Yeah, it's uh, it's a gift. And we all have different gifts. And I do believe that saying "thank you" is one of the greatest things that people can do. And I worry about those who don't feel the necessity of giving thanks—that that isn't important. I think it's one of the most important things that there is. "*Eucharisteo*" in Greek is "thanksgiving."

And, you know, I'd like to thank you for what you're making available to people for years and years to come. If anybody wants to study this field, they'll have, just, a marvelous resource in your archives. And something had to prompt you to invest so much of yourself in this project. And to be able to recognize that and to give thanks for it, well I'd just like you to know that, that I do.

HERMAN: What has been your greatest challenge?

ROGERS: Greatest challenge. [*pauses and thinks*] I suppose, to walk through the door and sing, [*sings*] "It's a beautiful day in this neighborhood," when I have had real sadness in my life. I had to go to Miami one hour after my father's funeral because they were having an M.R. day there that they said could not be cancelled. This was a personal appearance. And I'll never forget: we had twenty-three fifteen-minute performances in one day. And I had to sing, "It's a beautiful day in this neighborhood," for each one of them. And I remember telling Johnny, I said, "I'll try." Johnny Costa was there, and the first time I started—just before, he was playing the music, you know; [*imitates the music*] I just started to bawl. And by the time he had finished the introduction, my eyes were wet, but I went out on the place, and started singing, "It's a beautiful day in this neighborhood," and did it for every one of those fifteen-minute things the whole day long, and got through it, and listened to what the kids had to say. One child put up his hand and said, "Mr. Rogers, I just wear diapers at night now." And that was a very big step in that child's life, and I knew, you know, I knew that Dad was in a good place, and it was just that—well, your question made me remember that, so. That was one of the hardest times.

But when you know that you can make a difference in somebody's life, and you may want to know how I answered that child, who said that to me. I said, "Well, it'll be up to you when you give them up at night." And the people in the room, I remember, were—at first they snickered. And I told the kid what an important thing he had shared with me. And then I said, "It'll be up to you when you give them up at night."

HERMAN: How important is it, as an adult, to be in touch with your childhood?

ROGERS: I think it's very important, especially if you want to be communicating with children; I think it's essential.

HERMAN: And how would you compare Mr. Rogers to some of your contemporaries? Uh, Captain Kangaroo, Mr. Wizard?

ROGERS: Bob Keeshan, who was Captain Kangaroo, and I have been in touch for many, many years. In fact, I was on his program, and he was on ours, I believe—long time ago. But I call him every New Year's Day, and we go over our lives for the past year. He is a great advocate for children. The speeches that he gives—I'm very impressed with what he means to children. He's on that national board of the American Academy of Pediatrics and so is Bill Isler, who is our president here at Family Communications.

I don't know how to compare our programs; I really don't. I think each one reflects who we are, and that's the good thing. That's the only way you can have variety, since each one of us is who we are and unique.

HERMAN: What is television's responsibility to children?

ROGERS: To give them everything that we possibly can to help them grow in healthy ways and help them to recognize that they can be angry and not have to hurt themselves or anyone else. That they can have the full range of feelings and express them in very healthy, positive ways.

HERMAN: Let's talk about the lighter side of Mr. Rogers. Describe your reaction to the many parodies that have followed you throughout the years. One of them: Johnny Carson—start with that one?

ROGERS: Yes. [*smiles*] I remember one time going out to be on *The Tonight Show with Johnny Carson*, and he said to me, "You know, Fred, we wouldn't do these parodies if we didn't like you." And I—at first I didn't realize what he meant, and somebody said to me, "Well, my goodness, he's making you famous." [*laughs*] What he meant was, that this was a form of flattery, I think. But he did it—most of them were done with very good, gentle humor, you know.

Eddie Murphy did that "Mr. Robinson's Neighborhood," and I remember meeting him. And he just threw his arms around me the first time he saw me, and he said, "The real Mr. Rogers." Now, there have been times that I haven't been very pleased about a certain kind of parody. And this was not something that I saw myself, but this was on a local station somewhere, and some of our viewers got in touch with us and told us about it. But evidently, this man, in an afternoon program, wore a sweater and sneakers, came on the air, and talked even more slowly than I do, and said—and this was supposed to be something funny for mothers to see. But you never know, a child may have seen it. And what he did was, he said, "Now, children, take your mother's hairspray, and your daddy's cigarette lighter, and press the buttons, and you'll have a blowtorch." Now, he thought that was funny, of course. Well, we were able to put a stop to that, but he would do a different tip like that every day, in the guise of Mr. Rogers.

But most of them are with the—Harvey Korman was one of the first ones to do anything that was a takeoff on our program. But, you know, it's part of the—it's part of the culture now. And, uh, Joanne was watching something the other night. It was a movie. What was that movie called? *Father's Day*. She had rented that movie. And right in the middle of that movie, one of the characters, Billy Crystal, said to Robin Williams, when he was describing the kind of father that he was, he said, "You're Mr. Rogers," and then just went on with the dialogue. So it's—we're in the fabric of the—of the American people.

HERMAN: How has your fame affected your family life?

ROGERS: Oh, well, I guess you'd have to ask my wife and two sons about that. But, you know, we've always done the same things that we did before—mighty simple lifestyle. But that's what I care about. I've told you: deep and simple, that's what matters. And my one son, my younger son, people would ask him, "What's it like to have Mr. Rogers for a father?" He said, "He's the only father I ever had."

HERMAN: Did they watch *Mister Rogers'* growing up?

ROGERS: They did. Yeah. And they particularly liked to come to the studio, and now my grandsons love to come to the studio, and they run all over the place—I'll bring them in on a Saturday, you know. When the neighborhood of Make-Believe is up or my room is up. They play with the trolley, they do what kids would normally do.

I had a wonderful e-mail today—I wish I had it with me—that came from my daughter-in-law, who has the two boys in Nantucket at the moment. And there was a message from the younger one, which he dictated, saying how much he missed me and "I pledge allegiance to the flag of the United States of . . ." he went the whole way through that; he had learned it, evidently, and he wanted to share that with me. But she said, this is verbatim. This is the message from Bubba, verbatim.

HERMAN: So you're on e-mail.

ROGERS: Oh, yes. Oh, yes, Joanne and I are both quite busily connected to e-mail now. You know, my wife is a concert pianist. She's part of a two-piano team: Rogers and Morrison. And she and Jeannine Morrison play concerts together all over the place, and they do master classes, colleges—everywhere. She was—Joanne was a student of Ernst von Dohnányi, who was a great Hungarian musician. And his grandson, Christoph, is now the conductor of the . . . or has been the conductor of the Cleveland Orchestra, for many . . . in fact, Christoph was the other usher in our wedding. I told you that Kurt Browning was in our wedding and so was Christoph. So we're . . . as you had surmised, music is essential to our being. And it's fun to hear Joanne practice.

And I play, and I don't play the way Joanne plays, but she says to me one time, you know, "I could go without playing the piano for months at a time, but I know you couldn't," and it's true, I couldn't.

HERMAN: You play every day?

ROGERS: Oh, yeah. In fact, there's one song—I'll play it for you when we're finished—there's one song that Johnny arranged. It's called "Isn't it Romantic": that very popular song, but he made this arrangement, and I memorized it. And it's as if I'm visiting with Johnny each time that I play it.

You know, we have pieces of the people that have cared about us all through our lives, and they're all part of us now. And so we represent, each one of us represents, so many investments from others. No one of us is alone.

HERMAN: Have you ever thought about retirement?

ROGERS: Oh, sure. But what would you retire to? I mean, I've got the greatest job in the world. And as long as I'm healthy, I'd like to be able to offer what I've been given.

HERMAN: Now, this is a difficult question to ask, but will *Mister Rogers' Neighborhood* continue after you're gone in some . . . way?

ROGERS: I don't know. I'd like to think that it could continue in being reshown. It would be fun to think of ways to use—in fact, the other day, I was thinking: wouldn't it be fun to have the puppets actually have costumes that would be life-size, that people could wear, and that could coach people in those voices. And they could be recreated in ways—I don't know, I mean there—the sky's the limit when creativity's involved.

HERMAN: One of the things you've always emphasized is that you will be back; you will come back. Have you ever done an episode where you've said that you won't, I mean . . . is there some way that you are going to tell children . . .

ROGERS: I think if we were still being . . . if we were still having a live program, that I would. But there's no way to do that if you're going to have this constant recycling of the programs. And these programs are timeless. They're sort of like *The Wizard of Oz*, you know, that can be read at any epoch. And so—while I've dealt with the death of the goldfish and how people feel about dying, I don't know how I would—I don't think that—I could have a special program. And maybe that would be important, to have a special program, because I have no fear of dying. And, you know, I would be very glad to talk with, with anybody, about the joy of going on. You know, what's next? It'll be fun, too. I have a great trust in God's constant care; this is just one chapter in a long, long book: this part that we call "being on Earth," you know?

HERMAN: How would you like to be remembered?

ROGERS: To be remembered, wow. [*pauses to think*] I heard of somebody who was very, very famous asking somebody else, "Do you think I'll be remembered?" [*laughs thoughtfully*] I was sorry that he had such misgivings about that, you know? I'd just like to be remembered for—for being a compassionate human being, who happened to be fortunate enough to be born at a time where there was this fabulous thing called television that could allow me to use all the talents that I'd been given. Yeah.

THERE GOES THE NEIGHBORHOOD: MISTER ROGERS WILL MAKE LAST EPISODES OF SHOW IN DECEMBER

INTERVIEW BY ROB OWEN
PITTSBURGH POST-GAZETTE
NOVEMBER 12, 2000

The beautiful days in *Mister Rogers' Neighborhood* will continue, but next month on the show's simple set, Fred Rogers will hang up his famous cardigan sweater for the last time.

Taping of the final five installments of the thirty-two-year-old series will wrap in December. When this last week of episodes airs in August 2001, Rogers and his Family Communications Inc. will have completed thirty-three seasons and almost one thousand episodes of what is the longest-running children's program airing nationally.

During an interview Thursday in his cozy, den-like office at WQED in Oakland, Rogers said the timing was right. Next year when production concludes, Pittsburgh's favorite Neighbor will celebrate his fiftieth year in television.

"It was a fairly simple, straightforward decision," he said. "Of course, I prayed about it."

He compared this decision to when he left a job at NBC in New York to come to Pittsburgh in 1953. His friends thought he was crazy. WQED wasn't even on the air yet. Then, as now, he had a feeling that it was what he should do.

"I don't like to be spooky about stuff, but I do think that

sometimes you feel inspired to make certain decisions," Rogers said. "I've never tried to make a decision that had to do with selfishness. I think we certainly have done the kind of work I have wanted to do for children and one of the avenues has been the *Neighborhood*. That will always be a part of who I am, and I trust it will always be a part of those who have grown up with it and will continue to."

Just don't use the "R" word.

"Retire? No, I'm not retiring," Rogers said. "There are so many things Family Communications is involved with."

Rogers has no intention of slowing down. His latest book was published just this month. *The Giving Box* ($12.95, Running Press) encourages families to talk about giving and receiving. More books are in the offing. Rogers said Running Press offered three pages of suggestions for future projects.

"When I started, television was the new medium . . . well, there are some new media now and they're taking more and more of my time."

Rogers is a big proponent of cyberspace. His website, www.misterrogers.org, was recently updated with the addition of a new section for parents and behind-the-scenes photos from the *Neighborhood*.

SHOW SPANS GENERATIONS

Rogers often encounters adults who grew up with the *Neighborhood* and now watch it with their own children or nieces and nephews or even grandchildren. That the show is handed down is important to Rogers.

"For people who have feelings about a classic to be able to offer it to the next generation makes it all the more important for the children," Rogers said. "They sense what [the adults who love them] bring to it. Children long to know that they belong and they take the hint from the people they love as to what the tradition of this particular family is, and it's a very powerful thing."

With a huge collection of *Neighborhood* episodes to draw from, the program will continue to air on PBS.

"I can't imagine a PBS without *Mister Rogers' Neighborhood*," said PBS president and CEO Pat Mitchell. "I know the member stations feel that way. He probably has the widest carriage of almost any program on public television."

When Rogers called her with the news, Mitchell said she "was very sad. I think that's the emotion most people are going to feel when they hear this. I was deeply emotional about it because my son grew up with *Mister Rogers*."

But Mitchell was heartened by Rogers' plans for the future and his "commitment to do whatever he can for public television. He can continue to be a very real presence."

And that's his plan.

"I have felt for a long time that the best thing we could do was develop a library of tapes that can be seen over and over again," Rogers said. "And so I really feel we have accomplished our mission with the *Neighborhood*, and I'm interested in doing other things."

What those other things are, Rogers isn't sure of yet. He said he's focused on the final episodes and on making them the best they can be before moving forward.

"I'd like to use the next few months to be creative in

deciding how to use the time that we have, and the opportunities seem limitless. When you're offered a smorgasbord of things, I think it's wise to have some silence and some calm and some time to ask for guidance. I know who's in ultimate charge, and I will always know that I'll be led in the right way and in the best direction."

He pointed to a frame on the wall, obscured by the sun's glare. A closer look revealed these words: "Life Is For Service." It's a photo of Rogers' favorite sign on a wall at Rollins College, his Florida alma mater.

"Those of us in broadcasting have a special calling to give whatever we feel is the most nourishing that we can for our audience," Rogers said. "We are servants of those who watch and listen."

A TELEVISION ICON

Robert Thompson, director of the Center for the Study of Popular Television at Syracuse University, said Rogers is part of a small pantheon who shaped the medium, and educational children's television in particular.

"Along with a very small group of people—Steve Allen from late night, Irna Phillips with soap operas, Ernie Kovacs with video art—Fred Rogers really understood what the medium of television was all about, what it could do, how it was this intimate forum that talked to you in the privacy of your own living room, and he grasped that very early on," Thompson said.

"There's something about that program, when you're in your little pajamas with feet attached to them and you're home in the comfort of your living room on the couch, that was so extraordinarily comforting and quiet. It went down like a nice hot bowl of soup."

Since 1980, Rogers has taped about fifteen new episodes a year, adding to the hundreds produced in the 1970s. Thompson said viewers are unlikely to notice when new episodes stop. A child could conceivably cycle through the entire *Neighborhood* library without seeing a repeat.

"It's not like the cancellation of *Seinfeld*, where you've got a continuing plot line," Thompson said. "It's not like there are cliff-hangers at the end of each season where Mr. McFeely is tied to the train track and the trolley is coming and kids are waiting to see what happens."

No, the last episode of *Mister Rogers' Neighborhood* won't offer any closure. It will be like any other episode. The last week of programs deal with art education and culminate in an arts festival. Lady Elaine Fairchilde sets herself up as a judge because she's curator of the Museum-Go-Round.

"I can't tell you the punch line of it all because it's just too wonderful, but suffice it to say, Lady Elaine really grows enormously," Rogers said, "and there is a very happy ending."

Not that anyone expects otherwise.

Happy endings are what Rogers returns to viewers who write to him. All viewers who write get a personal response, even a seventeen-year-old named Tyler, who wrote and asked, "In your younger years, did you get a lot of chicks because you were Mr. Rogers?"

"I never want to be so busy that I can't answer the mail," Rogers said. "That is one of my biggest concerns. Usually we're a month or two behind, but we answer every letter that comes in, and now we have more than ever because of e-mail through the website."

KEEPING BUSY

In addition to more time to spend answering mail, Rogers has other projects to keep up with.

Mister Rogers' Neighborhood inspired a hands-on exhibit, created by the Pittsburgh Children's Museum with Family Communications. The exhibit is touring the country.

Earlier this month, *The Sky Above Mister Rogers' Neighborhood* opened at the Carnegie Science Center. Written by Rogers, it's a preschoolers' planetarium program that, for the first time, recasts the show's characters (voiced by Rogers) as virtual 3D images who shed light on what happens when it gets dark. Rogers said characters from the Neighborhood of Make-Believe will live on through multimedia productions like this one, books and possibly even a network radio show.

WQED president George Miles praised Rogers for exploring new avenues.

"The thing Fred and FCI have done with this whole Science Center exhibition is to think about a whole different form of distribution," Miles said. "I think it's going to be terrific. It's another way of getting the message out about the *Neighborhood.*"

Miles said *Mister Rogers' Neighborhood* will continue to

air on WQED/WQEX "for a long time. I think of it as Fred moving from one phase to another. I don't think of it as him retiring."

Nor do those closest to him. Rogers came to this decision several months ago, but only this week told his sister, Nancy Elaine Crozier (that's where the name "Lady Elaine" came from) of Latrobe.

"My sister then called [my wife] Joanne, and she said, 'Does that mean you all are going to slow down and travel some?' And Joanne says, 'I haven't seen any change whatsoever.'"

His schedule of speaking engagements remains booked through 2002.

"I received a letter today asking if I'd do a baccalaureate November 27 of 2001 and I looked in my book, and I have a commencement that day," Rogers said. "Everything we've talked about gives you the idea that this is not stopping."

Family Communications will continue to produce not-for-broadcast parenting and teaching videos and curriculum to accompany new projects. David Newell, who plays Mr. McFeely and has worked with Rogers since 1967, will still make "speedy delivery" visits to PBS member stations.

"Fred has written 95 percent of these shows himself," Newell said. "He's sort of the funnel we all go through."

Newell said he's been so busy he hasn't had time to think about the last taping, but he said he'll miss the performance work and the show's "studio family."

Today *Mister Rogers' Neighborhood* is seen on more than three hundred public television stations, plus the Armed Forces Network around the world and via cable in Canada, the Philippines, Guam and additional Asian countries.

Evidently, Rogers' voice got dubbed in some of those places. Newell, who doubles as FCI's director of public relations, recalled a breakfast in Texas twenty years ago when a waiter approached Rogers and said, "You speak beautiful Chinese."

Actually, Rogers speaks beautiful English, slowly, properly and with clear enunciation. Newell said singer Ricky Martin recently told Rosie O'Donnell he learned to speak English watching *Mister Rogers' Neighborhood*. Newell said *Neighborhood* tapes are used in Japan to teach English as a second language.

HEALTH NOT A FACTOR

At seventy-two, Rogers remains spry, still swimming every day. He's seeing a chiropractor for a leg injury that he sustained after tripping over a wire and falling while in Nantucket this past summer. Rogers was holding a casserole someone had given him and he didn't want it ruined, so he went down with the dish.

"I was sore for days," Rogers said, adding that he still has pain in one leg. "My chiropractor says this is just a transitory thing: 'Keep up your swimming, you'll be fine.'"

He's quick to offer further reassurance that he's in good health.

"My mother's side of the family lives forever," Rogers said. "I remember my great-grandmother and she was over one hundred. How old was I when she died? I think I was fourteen. She and my grandmother and my mother and I used to play rummy together. I found out years later that my grandmother and mother used to let me win one game and let Great Grandmother win the next game because these two ends of the spectrum wanted to win so badly."

Family Communications, which rents space at WQED's headquarters in Oakland, probably boasts the most loyal and loving staff in all of Pittsburgh—and perhaps television. Rogers' colleagues protect, respect and seem to genuinely care for the man who has become a cultural icon.

When associate producer Hedda Sharapan called Newell from an education conference in Atlanta this week and learned a reporter was visiting, she was eager to share some of her experiences. She said a Texas researcher called Rogers his hero and told an audience, "The only good thing kids can watch on television is *Mister Rogers.*"

There seems to be no person who has encountered Rogers who has not been touched by his gentle, caring manner. At public ceremonies, he often asks for a moment of silence so audience members can thank the people who made them who and what they are. It never fails to move people.

In a recent interview with *Newsweek* (most of which appeared on the magazine's website), Rogers was asked if it's true that he's not playing a character on television but simply playing himself. "One of the greatest gifts you can give anybody is the gift of your honest self. I also believe that kids can spot a phony a mile away."

As for the show's longevity, he said: "I do think that it has to do with offering yourself. I'm like you see me on the *Neighborhood.* People long to be in touch with honesty and with another human being that they feel is real, rather than a show."

Over the years, Rogers has hosted many celebrity guests, including LeVar Burton, David Copperfield, Tony Bennett, Lynn Swann, Wynton Marsalis, Stomp, Margaret Hamilton, Julia Child and locals like Bill Strickland of the Manchester Craftsmen's Guild.

And, of course, there's Yo-Yo Ma, a visitor to the *Neighborhood* several times.

"He's such a special man," Rogers said. "Aside from his being a superb cellist, he's just a wonderful human being. To be able to offer that kind of a person and that artistry to children who might not be able to be in touch with that personally, it's a real thrill for me."

Yet for all the celebrities, Rogers also remembers visits from unknowns. Just this past week a disabled child who could hardly speak visited the *Neighborhood* and sang with Mr. Rogers.

"I was walking this far off the ground," Rogers said, smiling at the memory and holding his hand a foot above the floor. "You know, there are special times and there are extra special times. I feel that the real drama of life is never center stage, it's always in the wings. It's never with the spotlight on, it's usually something that you don't expect at all."

HONORED MANY TIMES

The list of awards presented to Rogers runs twenty-five single-spaced, typed pages and includes lifetime achievement awards from the Daytime Emmys and the Television Critics Association. Rogers was named one of the "50 greatest

TV stars of all time" by TV Guide in 1996, got a star on the Hollywood Walk of Fame in 1998 and was inducted into the Television Hall of Fame in 1999.

Fred McFeely Rogers was born in Latrobe in 1928. After graduating from college in 1951, Rogers landed a series of TV positions, with *NBC Opera Theater*, *The Voice of Firestone*, *Lucky Strike Hit Parade* and *The Kate Smith Hour*. He did any number of jobs, from fetching coffee and Coke to working as a floor manager and orchestrating action behind the cameras.

It was the fledgling WQED and *The Children's Corner*, which debuted in April 1954 with host Josie Carey, that brought him to Pittsburgh. He produced the program, did the music and worked the puppets—including Daniel S. Tiger and King Friday XIII.

After moving to Canada to create a fifteen-minute children's show called *Mister Rogers*, he returned to WQED to develop a new half-hour format of *Mister Rogers' Neighborhood*. PBS began distributing it nationally on Feb. 19, 1968.

In that landmark inaugural episode, Rogers walked through the front door of his television house, doffed his raincoat and suit jacket and donned a sweater—button down, not zipped like the red one he would donate to the Smithsonian Institution. The routine established that day is designed to give children a sense of security. Rituals help them know what to expect and to settle in for Rogers' "television visit," as he calls it.

Rituals were part of Rogers' childhood visits with his beloved grandfather Fred Brooks McFeely, the namesake of the *Neighborhood*'s Mr. McFeely. Even today Rogers loves to talk about his grandfather, remembering how every Sunday as a child, he visited "Ding Dong," a nickname McFeely was christened with by his grandchildren.

"Invariably, he would say something when we left that was very much like what I say to the children," Rogers said. "He'd say, 'You know, you've made this day a special day just by being yourself.' It's been a privilege to pass on the good stuff that was given to me, and television has really been a fine vehicle for that. And now there are some other vehicles."

And then it hits him. As Rogers finishes the final *Neighborhood* episodes and thinks about the future, he realizes something about ol' Ding Dong.

"It just dawned on me. Mr. McFeely loved to start new things. Isn't that interesting?" Rogers said, pondering it a moment before he continued. "He helped to start practically every industry in Latrobe, but he always got out of it the minute it was going well so he'd have enough to invest in a new company. I remember in his eighties he decided he was going to have a chicken farm, so he bought five thousand chickens. When he got all that going, then he did something else. He didn't have a lot of money when he died, but he has this whole legacy of things that were started."

Rogers is a starter, too. His legacy is starting children off in life with warmth, appreciation and the reassuring words, "I like you just the way you are."

After three decades of *Mister Rogers' Neighborhood*, the feeling is most definitely mutual.

Post-Gazette Staff Writer Barbara Vancheri contributed to this article.

THE LAST INTERVIEW: *THE MISTER ROGERS' PARENTING BOOK*

INTERVIEW BY DIANE REHM
THE DIANE REHM SHOW
DECEMBER 17, 2002

DIANE REHM: Thanks for joining us. I'm Diane Rehm. Most of you know Fred Rogers as the host of *Mister Rogers' Neighborhood*, the children's television program that's been seen for more than three decades on Public Television stations. Fred Rogers is also an ordained minister, a student of child development, and a father and grandfather. All these experiences are shared in his new book, *The Mister Rogers' Parenting Book*, and he joins us this hour from the studios of WQED in Pittsburgh.

FRED ROGERS: Good morning, Diane Rehm. I'm pleased to talk with you, too, here from Pittsburgh and the Neighborhood of Make-Believe.

REHM: You know, I think you and I may have the two slowest voices in broadcasting.

ROGERS: Well, don't you think we need some slowness?

REHM: I do, I do.

ROGERS: Some deep, deep and simple times.

REHM: Exactly.

ROGERS: In this life.

REHM: You know, our forty-two-year-old son was in town yesterday because we were cooking together. And I mentioned to him that you were going to be on the program this morning and asked whether he remembered that I used to save my ironing till the end of the day so that he, his sister, and I could all watch your program together and indeed he did. What a delight your program is.

ROGERS: Well, thank you, and it's a treat to know that you and your family grew up with us.

REHM: Absolutely. I understand that the very first time you saw television, you were not very impressed.

ROGERS: Well, no, I saw it when I was a senior at Rollins College and I was home for the Easter holiday, and I just saw people throwing pies in each other's faces. And I thought, you know, if this medium is going to be in everybody's home, and, of course, at that time, it was in very few people's homes, I thought, this could be used for a lot better than that. And so I was all set to go to seminary as soon as I graduated from college. And I said to my parents, you know, I think I'd like to try television. And they said, "What?"

REHM: Yeah.

ROGERS: You've never even seen it. And I said, well, I've seen enough of it to know that I'd really like to put my hand in it.

REHM: And actually, in college, you also majored in music composition.

ROGERS: Yes. And so I was able to write all the songs for the *Neighborhood*, you know. I'm sitting by the piano right here at the WQED . . .

REHM: Oh, I hope you'll keep playing for us.

ROGERS: Oh, thanks. Tell me about your son.

REHM: Our son is a professor of philosophy at a college in Emmetsburg, Maryland, called Mount Saint Mary's.

ROGERS: Uh-huh.

REHM: And our daughter, who is thirty-eight, is a physician, and she works at the Lahey Clinic outside Boston.

ROGERS: Wow. You must be mighty proud of them.

REHM: You bet I am. And I believe that one of the reasons they are such good and decent human beings is that they did glean from your programs those values of kindness and caring and gentleness toward other people. For you, that must have been something that was truly elemental in your makeup.

ROGERS: I had wonderful parents, Diane, and grandparents. And I even knew my great grandmother. And I think that the fruit doesn't fall terribly far from the tree, and my parents always seemed to be thinking about other people. And my grandparents, during the 1918 flu epidemic, they got a group of people together and set up, in the armory of the small town where we all lived, an auxiliary hospital because the main hospital was completely filled with the people who had flu. And it was things like that, I mean, my grandfather said, "Well, you just can't have people—you just can't have sick people sitting out in the street."

REHM: So they really passed on to you that sense of the obligation that we, as human beings, have for each other. I understand you suffered several illnesses as a young child. Can you tell us about that?

ROGERS: Oh, just all those childhood diseases. You know, I had practically every one of those. And you were quarantined in those days.

REHM: I remember.

ROGERS: You had to stay in your bed in the house.

REHM: And you had the curtains drawn for fear, especially with measles, that you might hurt your eyesight.

ROGERS: Exactly. And it was during those times that I would make up all kinds of stories with the toys that I had, you know, little miniature figures, I'd have them all over the bed. I'm sure that was the beginning of the Neighborhood of Make-Believe, you know. You may remember King Friday XIII. [*as King Friday XIII*] It was a—it's with great pleasure that I speak with you today, Ms. Rehm, yes. [*as Queen Sarah*] And I certainly am pleased to be in your neighborhood, Diane Rehm. This is Queen Sarah speaking.

REHM: Of course it is. How nice to meet you.

ROGERS: [*as Queen Sarah*] Thank you. Oh, I see X the Owl up in the air. Just a moment. Oh, X, come talk with Diane Rehm. [*as X the Owl*] I always wanted to meet you, Diane. This is X the Owl.

REHM: Well, I'm so pleased to meet you.

ROGERS: [*as X the Owl*] Well, thanks, and my neighbor is Henrietta Pussycat. Just a second, I'll get her. [*knocking; as Henrietta Pussycat*] Meow. [*as X the Owl*] Hey, Hen, come on out here. [*as Henrietta Pussycat*] Meow, meow, meow, meow. Yes, it's Diane Rehm. Meow, meow, Diane Rehm. Meow, meow love meow program.

REHM: Oh, Meow, you're just marvelous. I'm so pleased to meet you.

ROGERS: [*as Henrietta Pussycat*] Meow, too. Meow, meow, meow, visit, meow, meow, meow, meow, meow. Well, that's for sure.

REHM: Oh, how wonderful. Well, actually, isn't that how you got your start in television? You started with a Public Television station there at WQED and helped to develop *The Children's Corner.*

ROGERS: Yes. And Josie Carey was the hostess, and Mrs. Dorothy Daniel was the general manager of the station. And the night before we went on the air, and that was in 1953, Mrs. Daniel gave us all favors at a party that she had. And the one favor she gave to me was a little tiger puppet. And I thought, oh, you know, we really should try to use that on the air just to show that we have affection for Mrs. Daniel. And so the next day, I said to Josie, "You know, we haven't planned to use puppets at all, but just for today, why don't I poke this little tiger through the back of the set, and we can call him Daniel in honor of Mrs. Daniel?"

ROGERS: And she said, "Oh, that'll be fine." So on that first program, I poked the little tiger through and said, [*as Daniel Striped Tiger*] "Hello, Josie, it's 5:04 and Columbus discovered America in 1493." And she said, "Well, Daniel, I'm so glad to meet you." And they talked for a little while, and I thought that would be the end of it. Well, that was just the beginning. And it's almost fifty years ago, Diane, that we did that.

REHM: Oh. That's just extraordinary. And . . .

ROGERS: And so Daniel . . .

REHM: . . . it was back in 1960, you see, that my first child was born, so I've been with you for many, many of those years. May I speak, Mr. Rogers, please, again to Meow, Meow?

ROGERS: [*as Henrietta Pussycat*] Meow, meow, meow, meow, Diane Rehm.

REHM: I so wanted to talk with you again because I didn't want you to leave without my letting you know how fond I am of kitty cats.

ROGERS: [*as Henrietta Pussycat*] Meow, meow, meow, pussy-cat, meow?

REHM: Exactly.

ROGERS: [*as Henrietta Pussycat*] Meow, meow, meow, Henrietta Pussycat, meow, meow name.

REHM: Exactly, Henrietta Pussycat. You are absolutely wonderful and I . . .

ROGERS: [*as Henrietta Pussycat*] Meow so glad.

REHM: Oh. And all your friends. You have so many friends around you, and friends are so important for little children, aren't they?

ROGERS: Isn't that so? I'm just—was thinking in the—talking about the parenting book, that there are so many different people who parent these days, you know. Not just mothers and fathers. Grandparents parent, aunts and uncles do parenting, childcare workers, babysitters, teachers, neighbors. There are so many people that I feel want to understand young children so that they can be all the more effective in their parenting.

REHM: And you know, for me, my husband and I have been married now for forty-three years, an anniversary we'll celebrate this week, but it seems to me that the two jobs for which we have the greatest obligations, and the two hardest jobs in the world, for which we have no training whatsoever are marriage and parenting. And for that reason, I'm awfully glad you've written your new book.

ROGERS: Well, thank you. I think that the only training that we have for them is that we grew up with parents, and so we often take on the role of those who parented us because—yeah.

REHM: And if they parented well, that's wonderful.

ROGERS: It's a blessing.

REHM: Of course. And then we can pass that on to our own children in that form. If, unfortunately, as we know, many too young people become parents without that kind of role modeling, then indeed it does have a problem. Mr. Rogers, we need to take just a short break here. And when we come back, we have so many callers who'd like to join this conversation. Will you be patient, please?

ROGERS: I certainly will and I'll welcome those who want to join with us.

REHM: Mr. Rogers, I'm so longing to hear one of your songs. I know that this year you delivered a commencement address at Dartmouth College where you sang one of your songs. I think you know which one I mean.

ROGERS: Oh, is it the one called, "It's You I Like"?

REHM: That's exactly right.

ROGERS: [*sings "It's You I Like"*] And it is you I like. Thank you.

REHM: Thank you. I would imagine that those Dartmouth students probably gave you a standing ovation for that song. We've had an e-mail from Ruth. She says, "Thank you, Mr. Rogers. My daughter, now seventeen years old, and I were devoted fans of yours. When she was four, I left the room momentarily and returned to find her gone and the television running. She was in her room, cleaning up. "Mr. Rogers says if you want to say I love you to your parents, you could clean your room." Several years later, when she announced she was too old for your show, I intended to write you and thank you because you were part of our family, and never did. So years tardy, here's my heartfelt thanks."

ROGERS: How generous of her to say that. But, you know, that comes from another song, Diane.

REHM: Oh, good.

ROGERS: "There Are Many Ways to Say I Love You." I won't sing it, but there are so many ways to say "I love you."

REHM: Are you sure you don't want to sing it?

ROGERS: Well, the middle part is [*sings*] "Cleaning up a room can say I love you / before you're asked to do it / Drawing special pictures for the holidays and making plays / You'll find many ways to say I love you / You'll find many ways to understand what love is / Many ways, many ways / Many ways to say I love you." [*talks*] Isn't that what life's all about, trying to find many different ways to say I love you.

REHM: Absolutely.

ROGERS: If the world could . . .

REHM: And we have another e-mail here from Falls Church, Virginia, from John who says, "I'm thirty-three now, but *Mister Rogers* was a huge part of my childhood. In fact, when I sat for the CPA exam a few years ago, Mom wrote Mr. Rogers about it. He responded with an autographed picture and a letter wishing me good luck. Mr. Rogers, you are special just because you're you."

ROGERS: Oh, John. What a marvelous memory. And to think that people can use the work that you've given over the air, I mean, that must give you great satisfaction, Diane, to know that there are those who are listening to your words and being nourished by them.

REHM: I so appreciate your saying that. You know, in fact, I've been doing this program now for more than twenty-three years, and we now have a second generation of listeners coming along, the children of those whose parents have listened to the program for years. So yes, you're right. It gives me great satisfaction, but it also makes me feel very humble to have had the opportunity to go into people homes, cars, and offices for all these years.

ROGERS: Yeah, you've been a radio neighbor to many.

REHM: You know, speaking of television, Mr. Rogers, many parents have been so concerned about the violent images on television. For example, the ones that are real, such as 9/11. What do you think parents can do to help their children make sense of those kinds of images?

ROGERS: It's very difficult with them being so pervasive. But I think the best thing we can do is, first, try to understand what our children are thinking, to try to be good listeners to begin with. I was listening to some children after the 9/11 catastrophe, and I was amazed to discover that many of them thought that that was happening every half hour of the day and night, because of the repeats on the—the news was being rebroadcast over and over again, and the children thought this was happening every, every minute. And they also— some of the very young ones, thought that it was happening in their town, not very far away. And so, I think the best thing we can do for very young children is to, first of all, try to understand what they're understanding of it is. But then, to let them know that we will do everything we can, as the adults in their life, to keep them safe. Even if we're scared, we are the adults, and we need to be strong as the children are growing. And let them know that we really will be in charge and we will keep them safe.

REHM: In your book, *The Mister Rogers' Parenting Book*, you talk a little about how children confront their fears through play.

ROGERS: Yes. I did that a lot when I was sick as a child. I made up all sorts of characters that could help me through those times. And I think that play is one of the most essential in-gredients of a child's life. And to be able to make up solutions through puppetry or any kind of imagery is an enormous help for a child. I loved being able just to give raw materials for play for children, just to see what they do with it.

REHM: You're talking about simple materials, such as puppets or blocks or that kind of thing.

ROGERS: Exactly. And things that the children can use to draw and make up the—do you know, Diane, that we have learned, in studying literacy, that one of the greatest helps in the development of literacy is dining room table conversation.

REHM: Indeed.

ROGERS: When children and adults get together to have dinner—and this doesn't happen all that often in our society, you know—they—there's a give and take. They learn new ideas. They learn new words. But the table conversation is just essential for helping children get ready to learn to read.

REHM: There are so many parents who are introducing computers at earlier and earlier ages with computer games and teaching that child to use a computer and seeing these images on the screens. What is your reaction to those very young children learning these computer games?

ROGERS: Well, there are some games that are quite educational and not scary. But there are many that are quite frightening. And I think that it's important for us to realize that we are the children's parents or grandparents or teachers, and let them know what we feel. You know, children long to belong. They want to know what their family stands for. They want to know what their school stands for. And even if they say, oh, I want to do this instead. When you say, you know, that's not the way our family works. This is who we are. I think they really love to know that they are part of something important.

REHM: At twenty-five before the hour, you're listening to *The Diane Rehm Show*. And let's go back to the telephones to Westminster, Maryland. Good morning, Rebecca, you're on the air.

REBECCA: I am just so thrilled and feel so privileged to get to speak to Mr. Rogers. I wanted to tell him about his effect on our autistic child. Back in the seventies, when he was in his toddler and later childhood ages there, he was so involved with himself and so removed from what was going on in the world around him, that the television could be on and all of his siblings excited and laughing and enjoying a program, and he would be sitting with his back to everyone and just self-absorbed. But when *Mister Rogers* came on, he would turn and sit and watch the television. And he listened and he connected with *Mister Rogers*. And I think that that was a starting point for him to become less involved with himself and more involved with some of the things that were around him. And he learned to listen and to enjoy other people and enjoy activities as the years went by. He is thirty—let's see—thirty-two now.

REHM: And how is he?

REBECCA: He is married. He has a son of his own who is the most beautiful grandchild in the world.

REHM: Oh, I'm so glad. That must make you very, very happy, Mr. Rogers, to hear that kind of comment.

ROGERS: Well, I must say that Rebecca's call is the greatest gift that I could have today. And I'm speaking in a halting way because I'm practically in tears. I didn't know her son personally. But to think that he grew up in a family that allowed him to become himself at a schedule in which he was able to become himself is, to me, such a blessing. And now you see that the—that he, having his own son, I bet he is a compassionate father.

REBECCA: He did. He learned compassion. Over the years, as he grows, he still learns that—when he learned compassion, it was so rewarding and so heartening to us. Because we had been told that most autistics never learn to have sympathy and to feel for others. And he does. He is a very tenderhearted boy now and a wonderful father. Oh, he loves that baby.

REHM: Oh, I'm so glad, Rebecca.

ROGERS: I hope you'll give hugs to both him and his little son.

REHM: How do you feel about the fact—and I must say I regard myself as at times a subject of ridicule because of my voice and because it is so slow and has such a wavery tone to it—how do you regard the fact that you have been made fun of, you've been mocked by some perhaps who've done it lovingly, but nevertheless, have made you a subject of their comedy.

ROGERS: Well, you know, at first, I thought, "I wonder why people do that, because each one of us is unique and that just happens to be who I am." But then, one day, I was at NBC in New York, and I was walking down the corridor, and the man who played on *Saturday Night Live* came out, and he was one of the people who did "Mr. Robinson's Neighborhood," you know, and he came out and said, "The real Mr. Rogers." This was Eddie Murphy. And he said, "Oh, the real Mr. Rogers," and he put his arms around me and gave me a big hug. And I thought, well, you really have been doing that with a lot of affection. And that happened also when I was with Mr. Carson, Johnny Carson, on his program one time, and he said, "You know, we've had these takeoffs about you, and I just want you to know that I would've never done it if we hadn't liked you."

REHM: Perfect.

ROGERS: We don't want to make somebody famous that we don't like.

REHM: Exactly. Oh, that's wonderful. All right, go ahead.

ROGERS: Do people do that—I mean, do people, do they do takeoffs on Diane Rehm?

REHM: Well, I have a voice problem, Mr. Rogers, it's called spasmodic dysphonia, and I have to have treatments to the vocal chords periodically. But I have to assume that, because I'm still on the air after all these years, that there is a growing tolerance, that there is an appreciation for the content of what we do rather than focusing so much on a problematic voice.

ROGERS: Well Diane, it's—it seems to me that it's exactly what we talk about on the *Neighborhood* all the time, and that is what's inside is far more important than what's on the outside. You know, Saint-Exupéry, in his book *The Little Prince*, said, *"Ce qui est essentiel est invisible pour les yeux."* What is essential is invisible to the eye. And he goes on to say that it's only with the heart that we see clearly.

REHM: Well, that moves right into this e-mail from Dennis, who says, "I am now in my final year of seminary to become a Catholic priest. I am currently a transitional deacon. God willing, I will be ordained priest in the spring. I believe growing up as a child knowing that Fred Rogers was a minister was a large influence in making my decision."

ROGERS: My, my, thank you for that, Dennis.

REHM: Isn't that lovely?

ROGERS: Wonderful.

REHM: And we have a caller in Ann Arbor, Michigan, Don, who'd like to speak with you. Good morning, sir.

DON: Good morning, Diane. Good morning, Fred.

ROGERS: Good morning, Don.

DON: One of the things, Fred, for which I respect you and for which I don't think you get enough credit is that you did not become a commercial sellout. You didn't endorse a line of clothing or games or toys, and while *Sesame Street* and *Barney* and the rest delivered generations of kids into the open arms of Kmart and Sears and so on, you did not, and I thank you for that.

ROGERS: Well, you're generous to mention that. There— as you can imagine, there have been opportunities for such things, but I've always felt that whatever we've produced, I would like it simply to be something that would extend the *Neighborhood* and to help people to use our work better, and that's why we've concentrated on recordings and books. And this latest book, I don't know whether you've seen it, Don, but it took us about fifty years to write it. I'm not being too facetious because all of the things that people have given us through the years, through their comments and their anec- dotes, I've tried to make this parenting book not only for mothers and fathers but for grandparents and childcare work- ers and all those who come in contact with very young chil- dren. I've wanted to give the legacy that—that really has been given to me through the years. I've worked with such wonder- ful people.

REHM: And now to Dallas, Texas, and to George. Good morning to you.

GEORGE: Good morning, Diane, and good morning, Mr. Rogers. Originally I called with the thought of asking why you decided early on to make music such a major part of how you communicate with people, but as I was sitting here listening to the discussion, I began to see a parallel in my life with yours. I, too, was sick early on, and I think a lot of what I am today I credit to that time when I had to be alone and be comfortable with myself and develop a sense of creativity. And I wonder if children today lose that with all the commercial games and commercial toys that are available and don't develop into their full potential because their sense of imagination isn't challenged. So basically it's really two questions, the music and the sense of imagination.

ROGERS: The music I think came from my grandfather. He just—his name was Mr. McFeely incidentally, and that's why we call our Speedy Delivery man Mr. McFeely. But my grandfather early on would teach us songs, and he played the fiddle, and I think that one of the most satisfying times of my life was when I was able to accompany him as he played—it was a song called, [*sings*] "Play gypsy, dance gypsy / play while you may / play gypsy tis a lovely . . ." I'll never forget that time.

REHM: Oh, it's a wonderful song.

ROGERS: And he would play the fiddle, and I would play the piano, but just the other night I was feeling a little blue, and I went to the piano, and I could literally laugh and cry through the tips of my fingers.

REHM: Why were you feeling blue?

ROGERS: Oh, I think it was just because I had a stomach ache. But I'm so used to good health, you know, that I like to be able to be strong and be able to do whatever the assignment is. And there are times when we realize hey, you know, we don't have to be perfect. And that's such a relief.

REHM: Absolutely. At seven minutes before the hour, you're listening to *The Diane Rehm Show*. Mr. Rogers, you . . .

ROGERS: You know, I didn't answer the rest of George's call.

REHM: Oh, forgive me, you're absolutely right, please go ahead.

ROGERS: Well, he was talking about these video games and things taking away the possibility of creativity. And I think that—I see it with my grandchildren. I think that they find different ways of expressing their creativity, and one of them just takes off and dances whenever he feels he needs to express himself. But he also is exceedingly adept at these little games, these video games. And so I think that we all find our own way, and I hope the children know that it's perfectly fine not to do the same thing that their neighbors are doing all the time. Life is a continuum and so are the ways of expressing life and creativity. There's—there's no perfect parent, there's no perfect child, but we all are human. And that's what I dedicate my work to.

REHM: You did not tape that last show with a sense of finality as far as somehow saying goodbye to those children.

ROGERS: Oh no.

REHM: I presume that was deliberate?

ROGERS: Oh yes. This—this library of tapes that we've developed, you know, we have about one thousand programs, it's really evergreen, and we deal with most of the major growth tasks of childhood in many different ways, and those programs can be used forever.

REHM: So they will go on. *Mister Rogers' Neighborhood* will be with another generation of children, at least. What would you like to play for us as we end our time together?

ROGERS: Well, I'd like to ask you. Would you like "A Beautiful Day in the Neighborhood," or would you like the song that we usually sing at the end, which is [*sings "It's Such a Good Feeling"*] It's such a good feeling / A very good feeling / The feeling you know that we're friends. [*talks*] And I feel that we are, Diane, thank you.

REHM: Oh, Fred Rogers, I have so looked forward to this hour and so enjoyed talking with you. I'm appreciative for your new book, *The Mister Rogers' Parenting Book*. I think it's going to help an awful lot of people, just as your program for all these years has been with and supported so many children. Thank you so much.

ROGERS: Thank you, Diane.

FRED ROGERS (1928–2003) was the creator, showrunner, and host of the internationally acclaimed children's television show *Mister Rogers' Neighborhood* which ran on PBS from 1968 to 2001. His work in children's television has been widely lauded, and he received over forty honorary degrees and several awards, including the Presidential Medal of Freedom in 2002, a Lifetime Achievement Emmy in 1997, and induction into the Television Hall of Fame in 1999. Rogers was also a musician, Presbyterian minister, and the author of several books for children and adults.

DAVID BIANCULLI is a guest host and TV critic on NPR's *Fresh Air* with Terry Gross. A contributor to the show since its inception, he has been a TV critic since 1975. From 1993 to 2007, Bianculli was a TV critic for the *New York Daily News*. Bianculli has written three books: *Dangerously Funny: The Uncensored Story of The Smothers Brothers Comedy Hour* (Simon & Schuster/Touchstone, 2009); *Teleliteracy: Taking Television Seriously* (1992); and *Dictionary of Teleliteracy* (1996). An associate professor of TV and film at Rowan University in New Jersey, Bianculli is also the founder and editor of the online magazine, TVWorthWatching.com.

JOHN PASTORE (1907–2000) was an American lawyer and politician. A member of the Democratic Party, he served as a United States senator from Rhode Island from 1950 to 1976 and as the governor of Rhode Island from 1945 to 1950. While a senator, Pastore headed the Joint Committee on Atomic Energy, held posts on the Commerce and Appropriations Committees and the Senate Democratic Policy Committee, and chaired the United States Senate Subcommittee on Communications.

TERRY GROSS started out in public radio in 1973 at WBFO, the NPR affiliate on the campus of her alma mater, the State University of New York at Buffalo. She became producer and host of *Fresh Air* in 1975, when it was still a local program. *Fresh Air* won a Peabody Award in 1994 for its "probing questions, revelatory interviews, and unusual insights." In 2003, Gross received public radio's highest honor, the Edward R. Murrow Award. She is the author of *All I Did Was Ask: Conversations with Writers, Actors, Musicians and Artists* (Hyperion, 2004).

PHILLIP HOOSE is the widely acclaimed author of books, essays, stories, songs, and articles, including the National Book Award–winning book, *Claudette Colvin: Twice Toward Justice* (Farrar, Straus and Giroux, 2009). A songwriter and performing musician, Hoose is a founding member of the Children's Music Network. He lives in Portland, Maine.

KAREN HERMAN is former vice president of collections and curatorial affairs at the Rock and Roll Hall of Fame and former vice president of the Television Academy Foundation archives. She is known for her work on *The Power of Rock* (2017) and The Interviews: An Oral History of Television (1997).

ROB OWEN is a television critic for the *Pittsburgh Post-Gazette* where he served as television editor from 1998 to 2010. He was a past president of the Television Critics Association, and currently freelances regularly for *Variety*, the *Seattle Times*, *Pittsburgh Magazine*, and the *Philadelphia Inquirer*. He wrote *Gen X TV: The Brady Bunch to Melrose Place* (Syracuse University Press, 1997) and was featured as a talking head in National Geographic Channel's *Generation X* (2016) and CNN's *The Nineties* (2017).

DIANE REHM hosted *The Diane Rehm Show*, distributed by NPR, from 1979 to 2016, when it had a weekly listening audience of two-and-a-half million. She now hosts a weekly podcast for NPR, *On My Mind*. She is the author of *On My Own* (Knopf, 2016) and *When My Time Comes* (Knopf, 2020). She lives in Washington, DC.

THE LAST INTERVIEW SERIES

RUTH BADER GINSBURG: THE LAST INTERVIEW AND OTHER CONVERSATIONS

"No one ever expected me to go to law school. I was supposed to be a high school teacher, or how else could I earn a living?"

$17.99 / $22.99 CAN
978-1-61219-919-1
ebook: 978-1-61219-920-7

MARILYN MONROE: THE LAST INTERVIEW AND OTHER CONVERSATIONS

"I'm so many people. They shock me sometimes. I wish I was just me!"

$16.99 / $21.99 CAN
978-1-61219-877-4
ebook: 978-1-61219-878-1

FRIDA KAHLO: THE LAST INTERVIEW AND OTHER CONVERSATIONS

"The only thing I know is that I paint because I need to, and I paint always whatever passes through my head, without any other consideration."

$16.99 / $21.99 CAN
978-1-61219-875-0
ebook: 978-1-61219-876-7

THE LAST INTERVIEW SERIES

TONI MORRISON: THE LAST INTERVIEW AND OTHER CONVERSATIONS

"Knowledge is what's important, you know? Not the erasure, but the confrontation of it."

$16.99 / 21.99 CAN
978-1-61219-873-6
ebook: 978-1-61219-874-3

GRAHAM GREENE: THE LAST INTERVIEW AND OTHER CONVERSATIONS

"I think to exclude politics from a novel is to exclude a whole aspect of life."

$16.99 / 21.99 CAN
978-1-61219-814-9
ebook: 978-1-61219-815-6

ANTHONY BOURDAIN: THE LAST INTERVIEW AND OTHER CONVERSATIONS

"We should feed our enemies Chicken McNuggets."

$16.99 / $21.99 CAN
978-1-61219-824-8
ebook: 978-1-61219-825-5

THE LAST INTERVIEW SERIES

URSULA K. LE GUIN: THE LAST INTERVIEW AND OTHER CONVERSATIONS

"Resistance and change often begin in art.
Very often in our art, the art of words."

$16.99 / $21.99 CAN
978-1-61219-779-1
ebook: 978-1-61219-780-7

PRINCE: THE LAST INTERVIEW AND OTHER CONVERSATIONS

"That's what you want. Transcendence.
When that happens—oh, boy."

$16.99 / $22.99 CAN
978-1-61219-745-6
ebook: 978-1-61219-746-3

JULIA CHILD: THE LAST INTERVIEW AND OTHER CONVERSATIONS

"I'm not a chef, I'm a teacher and a cook."

$16.99 / $22.99 CAN
978-1-61219-733-3
ebook: 978-1-61219-734-0

THE LAST INTERVIEW SERIES

KURT VONNEGUT: THE LAST INTERVIEW

"I think it can be tremendously refreshing if a creator of literature has something on his mind other than the history of literature so far. Literature should not disappear up its own asshole, so to speak."

$15.95 / $17.95 CAN
978-1-61219-090-7
ebook: 978-1-61219-091-4

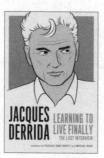

JACQUES DERRIDA: THE LAST INTERVIEW
LEARNING TO LIVE FINALLY

"I am at war with myself, it's true, you couldn't possibly know to what extent... I say contradictory things that are, we might say, in real tension; they are what construct me, make me live, and will make me die."

translated by PASCAL-ANNE BRAULT and MICHAEL NAAS

$15.95 / $17.95 CAN
978-1-61219-094-5
ebook: 978-1-61219-032-7

ROBERTO BOLAÑO: THE LAST INTERVIEW

"Posthumous: It sounds like the name of a Roman gladiator, an unconquered gladiator. At least that's what poor Posthumous would like to believe. It gives him courage."

translated by SYBIL PEREZ and others

$15.95 / $17.95 CAN
978-1-61219-095-2
ebook: 978-1-61219-033-4

THE LAST INTERVIEW SERIES

JORGE LUIS BORGES: THE LAST INTERVIEW

"Believe me: the benefits of blindness have been greatly exaggerated. If I could see, I would never leave the house, I'd stay indoors reading the many books that surround me."

translated by KIT MAUDE

$15.95 / $15.95 CAN
978-1-61219-204-8
ebook: 978-1-61219-205-5

HANNAH ARENDT: THE LAST INTERVIEW

"There are no dangerous thoughts for the simple reason that thinking itself is such a dangerous enterprise."

$15.95 / $15.95 CAN
978-1-61219-311-3
ebook: 978-1-61219-312-0

RAY BRADBURY: THE LAST INTERVIEW

"You don't have to destroy books to destroy a culture. Just get people to stop reading them."

$15.95 / $15.95 CAN
978-1-61219-421-9
ebook: 978-1-61219-422-6

THE LAST INTERVIEW SERIES

JAMES BALDWIN: THE LAST INTERVIEW

"You don't realize that you're intelligent until it gets you into trouble."

$15.95 / $15.95 CAN
978-1-61219-400-4
ebook: 978-1-61219-401-1

GABRIEL GÁRCIA MÁRQUEZ: THE LAST INTERVIEW

"The only thing the Nobel Prize is good for is not having to wait in line."

$15.95 / $15.95 CAN
978-1-61219-480-6
ebook: 978-1-61219-481-3

LOU REED: THE LAST INTERVIEW

"Hubert Selby. William Burroughs. Allen Ginsberg. Delmore Schwartz... I thought if you could do what those writers did and put it to drums and guitar, you'd have the greatest thing on earth."

$15.95 / $15.95 CAN
978-1-61219-478-3
ebook: 978-1-61219-479-0

THE LAST INTERVIEW SERIES

ERNEST HEMINGWAY: THE LAST INTERVIEW

"The most essential gift for a good writer is a built-in, shockproof shit detector."

$15.95 / $20.95 CAN
978-1-61219-522-3
ebook: 978-1-61219-523-0

PHILIP K. DICK: THE LAST INTERVIEW

"The basic thing is, how frightened are you of chaos? And how happy are you with order?"

$15.95 / $20.95 CAN
978-1-61219-526-1
ebook: 978-1-61219-527-8

NORA EPHRON: THE LAST INTERVIEW

"You better *make* them care about what you think. It had better be quirky or perverse or thoughtful enough so that you hit some chord in them. Otherwise, it doesn't work."

$15.95 / $20.95 CAN
978-1-61219-524-7
ebook: 978-1-61219-525-4

THE LAST INTERVIEW SERIES

JANE JACOBS: THE LAST INTERVIEW

"I would like it to be understood that all our human economic achievements have been done by ordinary people, not by exceptionally educated people, or by elites, or by supernatural forces."

$15.95 / $20.95 CAN
978-1-61219-534-6
ebook: 978-1-61219-535-3

DAVID BOWIE: THE LAST INTERVIEW

"I have no time for glamour. It seems a ridiculous thing to strive for... A clean pair of shoes should serve quite well."

$16.99 / $22.99 CAN
978-1-61219-575-9
ebook: 978-1-61219-576-6

MARTIN LUTHER KING, JR.: THE LAST INTERVIEW

"Injustice anywhere is a threat to justice everywhere."

$15.99 / $21.99 CAN
978-1-61219-616-9
ebook: 978-1-61219-617-6